END

MW01286741

Working in the publishing world for 20 years, I have read hundreds of manuscripts. Also, I have read hundreds of books over the years. Some of these books have been boring, redundant, and way too religious for my taste. However, that is not the case with S. J. Hill's book, *A Love for the Ages*. Hill takes us on a journey that began in an ancient garden. He reminds us that the Bible is a love story, from beginning to end. A great romance writer makes us believe in love and romance. This is exactly what *A Love for the Ages* has done. Hill restores the original theme of love and romance in the greatest story ever told. He also exposes some of the legalistic, ascetic, and philosophical influences that have sought to break up the divine marriage. In the end, he makes me believe that this love is real and available for all of us.

Don Milam, Acquisitions Editor, Whitaker House, and author of *The Ancient Language of Eden*.

S. J. Hill, who I first met teaching believers to *enjoy* God, takes us deeper into the extravagant affections of God in his book, *A Love for the Ages*. S. J. introduces us to the divine romance of Scripture and to the One who is our passionate and faithful Bridegroom. I'm thrilled to see another treatise that genuinely represents God as consistent love in His very essence.

Dr. Bradley Jersak, Faculty of N. T. & Patristics, Westminster Theological Centre, and author of *Can You Hear Me?* and *Her Gates Will Never Be Shut*.

S. J. Hill rips the Old Testament from the hands of the legalists and places it in the heart of the divine lover of the human race. The covenant is not an accidental footnote to the biblical story; it is the heartbeat of the Book, beginning with the relationship of the Father, Son, and Spirit in eternity and stretching to the marriage supper of the Lamb at the consummation of the ages. For those of us who are troubled by the "glaring difference" between the God of the Old Testament and the Lord Jesus Christ, Hill's *A Love for the Ages* is a great place to start.

> C. Baxter Kruger, Ph.D., and author of *The Great Dance*, *Across All Worlds*, and the international bestseller, *The Shack Revisited*.

In his new book, *A Love for the Ages*, S. J. does a brilliant job of capturing the tender heart of God that is woven throughout the pages of the Bible. I was greatly encouraged to discover many new nuggets of revelation especially found in the Old Testament that powerfully illustrate His all-consuming love for us. Whether you are wanting to know more of God's love as Father or the love of Jesus as our passionate Bridegroom, this book is a must read.

> Barry Adams, Father Heart Communications, and author of *Father's Love Letter*.

In *A Love for the Ages*, S. J. Hill identifies and follows a thread that weaves its way throughout Scripture—God's passionate love for humanity and His active pursuit of man through history. S. J.'s deliberate exploration of the language and symbolism of the divine courtship and matrimony between God and human beings found in the biblical narrative will capture your imagination! As I read *A Love for the Ages*, I found myself embraced and captivated by the affections of God. I believe you will be too.

> Russ Hewett, Senior minister – Grace Church, Bangor, Maine.

In *A Love for the Ages*, S. J. Hill unveils the passionate love of God revealed in the paradigm of marriage that is woven throughout the biblical narrative and now fully unveiled in Christ. He has always taken the initiative to woo us into sharing life in living union with Him. This book will renew your heart and spark your relationship with Jesus!

Rod Williams, Pastor – Kainos Santa Cruz.

There is revelation in this manuscript that will awaken and fuel our passions for Jesus Christ.

Francis Frangipane, Pastor and author of the best-selling book, *The Three Battlegrounds.*

S.J. Hill has managed to bring a fresh understanding to a topic that so desperately needs a renewal in the body of Christ. The divine romance and passion of the Father for all that is His is found on every page of this book. The overwhelming theme of Scripture is the Father's love for His people, a truth that gets lost in all our theologizing and historicity. This book will rekindle a love affair with the Father for anyone who has lost that feeling of his or her "first love."

Caleb Miller – Pastor, recording artist, and author of *The Divine Reversal.*

A Love for the Ages

from the author of

Enjoying God

S. J. Hill

Father's House Press

A LOVE FOR THE AGES by S. J. Hill

Father's House Press
P. O. Box 188
Timnath, CO 80547

ISBN: 978-0-9916265-2-6

Unless otherwise noted, Scripture quotations are taken from the Holy Bible, New International Version (NIV). Copyright © 1973, 1978, 1984 by International Bible Society. Used by permission of Zondervan Publishing House. All rights reserved.

Scripture quotations marked (NASB) are taken from the New American Standard Bible. Copyright © 1960, 1977, 1995 by the Lockman Foundation. Used by permission.

Scripture quotations marked (NKJV) are taken from the New King James Version. Copyright © 1970, 1980, 1982 by Thomas Nelson, Inc. Used by permission. All rights reserved.

Formerly published by Relevant Books in 2005 under the title of *Burning Desire*.

Cover design by Caleb Miller

Visit the author's website at www.sjhillonline.com. He can also be contacted at stephenhill6@gmail.com.

Printed in the United States of America

ACKNOWLEDGMENTS

Any time you write a book, it's imperative to remind yourself that your work is really a by-product of the influence of a lot of different individuals. I readily admit that a number of people have had a profound effect on my life and writings—family, friends, and the authors I love. No doubt you will find some of their thoughts and ideas in this book. I only wish I had the space to acknowledge each of them. I do, however, want to thank a few people to whom I am indebted.

To my Mom and Dad: Thank you for your godly example over the years. Just to know that you loved me and were proud of me means more to me than you will ever know.

To Bill Stevenson: Thank you for letting me live in your fabulous home in Hawaii during the finishing of this book. What an inspiration it was for me to be able to write while surrounded by the beauty of the Pacific Ocean and volcanic mountains on the island of Kauai.

To Arlene Sloan: Thanks for your incredible generosity and support. Pam and I truly love you and value your friendship.

To Clyde Stutzman, Steve Wise, Warren Walters, David Rhodes, Scott Vanderhoof, Stephen Crosby, Russ Hewett, Brad Jersak, Ron Allen, Mike Lechlitner, Dan Hardway, and Brent Byrnes: Thanks for your friendship and the good times we've shared together. I've loved laughing with you guys.

To my sons, Jonathan and Lance: Thanks for always reminding me not to be "religious" in my approach to life.

You are the joy of my life. I'm proud of you and love you beyond words!

To Pam, my wife: I dedicate this book to you. You are my bride and my partner on the journey into God's heart. Thanks for your help in editing this book. I will always love you!

Finally, to all the men and women who have befriended me over the years: It has been a wild ride, but I am honored to be called your friend.

CONTENTS

INTRODUCTION

Although I was raised in church by good Christian parents, I still grew up afraid of God. This was due, in part, to having been "dangled over hell" by preachers more times than I choose to remember. I was also warned repeatedly that when I died I would stand before God, and He would judge me for my "lack of commitment" and expose all my shortcomings for everyone to see.

Does any of that surprise you? Maybe some of you can identify with my experience. While I had been told numerous times that God loved me, I never really felt that He liked me. In fact, He seemed rather distant and difficult to please. Because I was continually haunted by a sense of never being able to do enough to satisfy Him, my fears were reinforced even more.

I was particularly troubled by my understanding of the God of the Old Testament, especially in light of the passages that spoke of His jealous anger and righteous judgments. And so, for the most part, I ignored those sections of the Bible altogether.

Still, I continued to plod along in my quest for spiritual reality. Even though I had come to believe that I could never measure up to what I thought God required of me, I tried surrendering my heart to religious rules and regulations. I really thought this was what He expected. After all, isn't that what the Ten Commandments are all about?

It wasn't until years later that I began to have my heart awakened to the beauty and passion of God and to the sacred romance of the ages. What I discovered not only fascinated me but also set me on a course that radically altered my Christian experience.

In the following pages, I want to introduce you to a side of God that many of you have never seen before. What you're about to read will change your way of thinking concerning who He is. You will not only be surprised but also intrigued as you discover unique aspects of God's personality that you didn't know existed.

God isn't anything like man-made religion has depicted Him. All too often He has been gravely misunderstood and misrepresented. Even His methods and motives have been called into question. Yet, God's passionate love for you is beyond your wildest imagination! Will you allow your heart to be awakened to the beauty of who He is and to the extravagant affections He has for you? Let me lead you on a path that will change your life forever. Trust me, I know.

Chapter One

A LOVE BEFORE
TIME BEGAN

Have you ever thought of the Bible as having one predominant theme—a common thread that runs from beginning to end? While it's true that as you read and study its pages you'll find many issues relating to the plan of redemption, the one thread that holds them all together is the bridal theme of Scripture. You may have read the Bible any number of times and never noticed it, but the Scriptures are filled with bridal language—everything from the *mysterious* union between a man and a woman to betrothals and weddings that foreshadowed an even greater love that would be revealed over time. Once you begin looking for the bridal theme, you'll be hard pressed to read through a book or two of the Bible without seeing it.

Think about it for a moment. God began human history with a wedding, and John, in the book of Revelation, introduces us to another wedding as well. While Genesis 2:21-25 vividly describes the sacred union between Adam and Eve, Revelation 19:7-9 beautifully depicts the sacred union between Christ and His bride. This isn't a coincidence at all. I am convinced that God's design is profoundly intentional, and it displays His passionate heart for the human race.

When we begin to recognize the bridal theme that is woven throughout the Bible, it will not only change the way we read Scripture, but it will also enable us to understand and experience the romance of redemption. Keep in mind, it was Jesus who said, "Now this is eternal life: that they may *know* you, the only true God, and Jesus Christ, whom you have sent" (John 17:3, italics added). The word *know* in the original Greek language is speaking of an intimate knowing. It's the same "knowing" in which Adam knew his wife Eve and husbands and wives have known each other ever since. God, who loves the human heart in ways we will never fully understand, is always seeking to draw us into a deeper, more intimate relationship with Himself.

IN THE BEGINNING—A GARDEN WEDDING

It's far too easy to look at the first few chapters of Genesis and read them as if they are just historical in nature. Yet, a deeply passionate Creator joyfully fashioned the universe and our solar system. He handcrafted this planet with tender loving care. He carefully designed the birds of the air and the fish of the sea to coexist in an incredible ecological harmony. The wonder and splendor of what initially took place is truly beyond description. Animals tasted their first bites of leafy vegetation. Birds spread their soft wings for a first flight. Flowers opened their tender petals for the initial exposure to sunlight. It was God's artistry put on display, and it was perfect in every way.

But Genesis tells us that God wasn't fully content with the creatures He had formed. His heart yearned for one more. He longed for a *being* with whom He could be intimate and to whom He could give Himself completely.

Genesis 1:26 reinforces this for us by stating that the Godhead said, "Let us make man in our image, in our likeness, and let them rule over the fish of the sea and the birds of the air, over the livestock, over all the earth, and over all the creatures that move along the ground."

So God fashioned a man in His own image to experience the pure pleasure of His presence. However, it appears that over time Adam mysteriously began to sense there was something missing in his own human experience. As he looked at the wild animals that surrounded him, he noticed that each had a male and female counterpart. I can only imagine that it awakened a longing within him that he couldn't fully explain. There was a desire in his heart for something or "someone" comparable to himself.

Genesis even tells us that at one point God looked at Adam's plight and said, "This isn't good." These words had never been uttered before. Up to that point, all we read in Scripture concerning creation are the words, "And God saw that it was good." Is it any wonder? Anything God created had to be good.

Yet, why was it that the only thing in all of creation that God said was "not good" was Adam's initial aloneness when he found himself without a suitable companion? Why did Adam feel strangely unfulfilled even though all he had known and experienced was perfect in every way? And what is the spiritual significance of what we read in Genesis 2:18 when God looked at Adam and said, "*It is not good* for the man to be alone. I will make a helper suitable for him" (italics added)?

In order to have these questions answered for us, we need to be reminded of something the Apostle Paul wrote in his first letter to the church at Corinth. In 1 Corinthians

15:45, Paul uniquely refers to Christ as "the last Adam." This comparison between Adam and Jesus has some far-reaching implications. That's why this verse takes on even greater significance for us when we look at it from a prophetic perspective.

Adam's seemingly unexplainable longing for "someone" can be traced back to the heart of the Father and an eternal promise He made to His Son to give Him a bride. There was something that God put in Adam's "DNA" that was to mirror the eternal longing in the heart of the Son of God for a partner suitable for Him. In other words, Adam would become a living illustration of the last Adam's pure desire for a bride.

Adam's desire for a suitable companion was to be an earthly reflection of the longing that was in the heart of the Son of God from before the beginning of time. It was the longing for a future wife whom His Father had chosen for Him.

What an astounding story! There has never been another like it. The mystery of it all—to think that God, who is perfect and complete in Himself, would have an eternal longing in His heart that could only be satisfied by embracing people from all the nations of the world who would one day be wed to Him. Who can comprehend it?

So when Genesis 2:24 says, "For this reason a man will leave his father and mother and be united to his wife, and they will become one flesh," we can now begin to understand that this verse is not only speaking of the union between a man and a woman but, in reality, is also speaking of what the Son of God was willing to do for His future bride.

Paul reiterates this truth for us in Ephesians 5:31-32. The Son left His Father and the splendor of all He had known in order to make a perilous journey to this tiny planet to win the hand of His future bride. This kind of love is beyond anything ever portrayed by Hollywood. It's the romance of redemption, and it's what God wants to use to awaken our hearts to the passion that burns deep in His heart for each one of us.

THE BRIDEGROOM GOD

As we trace the bridal theme into the New Testament, we discover that the eternal romance between God and human beings continues to crescendo. For example, in Matthew 9:15, Jesus unveiled His true feelings and intentions when He referred to Himself as a bridegroom. He said to the disciples of John the Baptist, "How can the guests of the bridegroom mourn while he is with them? The time will come when the bridegroom will be taken from them; then they will fast."

Think of the significance of such language. Jesus was not only speaking of His life's mission as the Bridegroom, but He was also using bridal terminology to convey His deepest feelings for mankind. He understood that there is something about romantic, passionate language that touches the heart like nothing else can.

Have you also considered that Jesus' first recorded miracle took place at a wedding? According to the second chapter of John, Christ was invited to attend a marriage ceremony in the village of Cana in Galilee. If you recall, Jesus' mother came to Him and informed Him that the wedding party was in a real predicament. For whatever reason—poor planning or a broken pot—they had run out of wine. Mary asked Jesus to do something about the situation. Do you remember His reply? He answered His mother with these words: "My time has not yet come" (John 2:4).

I have spent some time reflecting on Jesus' answer, which, at first glance, appears a little curt. But in the process of my studies, I have discovered something very interesting. In Jesus' day, it was always the bridegroom who prepared the wine for the wedding celebration. It was the bridegroom's responsibility to make sure there was sufficient wine for all the guests.

I believe when Jesus said, "My time has not yet come," He wasn't suggesting that it was His Father's will for Him to wait for a more opportune time to begin His miracle ministry. Instead, I truly think Jesus was speaking as a bridegroom and of a time when He would provide the wine for His own wedding day—the marriage supper of the Lamb (Rev. 19:7).

When Jesus eventually turned the water into wine, He was giving us a glimpse into what it would be like at the celebration of His wedding when He would save the best "wine" for last (John 2:9-10). One can only imagine the anticipation and excitement that Jesus must have felt!

In Revelation 21:1-2, John writes, "Then I saw a new heaven and a new earth, for the first heaven and the first earth had passed away, and there was no longer any sea. I saw the Holy City, the new Jerusalem, coming down out of heaven from God, prepared as a bride beautifully dressed for her husband."

Even now, the Holy Spirit is wooing and calling us to experience a deeper intimacy with Jesus than what we've ever known before. He is awakening our hearts to the Lord's goodness and to the reality that we have been adorned in the radiant splendor of Christ's beauty and clothed with His perfections. He is continually reassuring us that one day we will see our Bridegroom face to face and enjoy the pure pleasure of being loved by Him.

So as you open your heart to the bridal theme of Scripture and as you begin to hear the wedding bells echoing through the pages, just remember that the One who has been ringing them before the beginning of time has chosen you for Himself.

CLOSING PRAYER

Father, in the Name of Jesus, I thank You for Your tender love for me. I thank You for choosing me by name before the foundation of the world to be a part of Your Son's bride. Jesus, I ask You to reveal Yourself to me as my Bridegroom so that I can experience the pleasures of Your heart. I want to know You more intimately. Amen.

Chapter Two

PORTRAITS OF THE
BRIDE AND GROOM

Several years ago, I had the privilege of assisting in the wedding of two of my former students. As my wife and I were sitting in the audience waiting for the bride to walk down the aisle, I had a rather unusual idea cross my mind. While the eyes of everyone else present were fixed on the spot where Lisa would make her grand entrance, I felt compelled to watch Mike's reaction as he saw his bride for the first time in her wedding gown.

The whole experience was somewhat surreal for me. As I stared at the intensity in Mike's eyes and the redness in his face as the veins popped out on his neck, I seemed to catch a glimpse of something that transcended what we were celebrating that day. For a brief moment, it was as if I had come face to face with the fiery passion of Jesus for His bride. I know this seems a bit odd, to say the least, but I found myself thinking about another wedding celebration (Rev. 19:7; 22:17).

As we have already seen, even before time began, there was always a burning desire in the heart of the Father to have a *partner* suitable for His Son. We were chosen and set apart so that one day He would have a bride who would be His eternal joy.

Once we understand that this has always been the Father's ultimate intention, we will be able to properly interpret God's dealings with man from the beginning. The creation of Adam and Eve, the history of Israel, the birth of Christ, as well as His death and resurrection will take on even greater significance for us.

The bridal theme is truly the heart of the Scriptures. In fact, the Bible is a passionate love story about a *holy romance* between God and human beings. The revelation of Jesus as the eternal Bridegroom is found throughout its pages. And it's the bridal perspective that will arouse our hearts to the beauty and poetry of the Bible and enable us to make sense of what we read.

ADAM AND EVE

As we return to the story of the first couple, we are reminded again that once upon a time, under the canopy of a bright blue, virgin sky, Adam and Eve were joined together in holy matrimony. It was God who had opened Adam's side and from it made a woman, and it was God who escorted Eve to her husband in the first celebration of marriage.

But, as we've already noted, this momentous occasion wasn't just about Adam and Eve. Their wedding was to foreshadow something that would take place centuries later that would have far greater eternal significance. The prophetic pictures illustrated for us in this wedding are deeply moving. As we reflect upon them, our hearts will be awakened more and more to the reality of the Lord's infinite love for each of us.

For example, we are told in 2 Corinthians 11:3 that it was Eve, not Adam, who was deceived by the serpent in the Garden. The serpent seduced Eve by getting her to believe that God couldn't be trusted and that He was withholding His best from her. Eve bought into the lie and was led blindly down a path that ended in death. Even so, Adam, with his eyes wide open, was willing to follow Eve into death because he couldn't imagine living without her.

Like the first couple, each of us has fallen prey to evil. Like Eve, each of us has been seduced by a lie. Yet Jesus, the last Adam, with His eyes wide open, willingly followed us into death because He couldn't stand the thought of living without us forever.

Furthermore, when we read in Genesis that God put Adam to sleep and from his side made a woman who was of his own flesh and bone, we are introduced to another powerful analogy. Although God's method for creating Eve appears rather strange in comparison to the way He formed the rest of creation, in reality, it's a prophetic picture of the bride of Christ formed from the open, wounded side of Jesus as He fell asleep in death. Jesus willingly identified with our humanity in order to elevate us to a sacred place of intimacy and partnership that would never end.

ISAAC AND REBEKAH

The Bible is truly an extraordinary love letter. Who can ignore the passionate language that echoes through its pages? And the theme is always the same—God is continually seeking to win the hand of human beings because of His burning love for them.

Like the story of Adam and Eve, the experience of Isaac and Rebekah stands out as another beautiful prophetic portrait of Christ and His bride. Yes, the love affair between Isaac and Rebekah was a true story of human passion and intrigue. However, what appears on the surface to be nothing more than a curious tale about a father's desire to find a wife for his son is really a striking illustration of God's passion to pursue people for the sake of His beloved Son.

The fact that Abraham's relationship with Isaac is a prophetic picture of the Father's relationship with Jesus can't be overstated. All we have to do is look at the supernatural birth of Isaac, as well as the compelling story of Abraham's willingness to give up his unique son in death, in order to discover the prophetic parallels (Gen. 21-22).

But the comparisons don't stop there. Abraham desired to find a bride for his son from among his own kindred people and not from the young women of Canaan, where he was living at the time. He, therefore, made his oldest and most trusted servant promise to go to his homeland in Mesopotamia to find a wife for Isaac (Gen. 24:2-4).

As the story unfolds, it soon becomes apparent that the servant's role is similar to the Holy Spirit's role in the earth. The servant took with him gifts from the father's house to woo the prospective bride. He set out on the long, difficult journey and eventually arrived at the city of Nahor, in the region of Mesopotamia.

It was there on the outskirts of the city that Abraham's servant met a beautiful, young woman. Rebekah came to a well near the city to draw water. Interestingly enough, the servant had just prayed that God would show him who was to be Isaac's bride. He had even asked the Lord for a sign so there would be no mistake as to who the young woman

14

would be. He had prayed that the woman who not only offered him a drink but also gave his camels some water would be the future wife for Isaac.

According to Genesis 24:17-20, when Abraham's servant asked Rebekah for a drink, she not only gave him a drink but provided water for his camels as well. He was astonished by what had just transpired and was overjoyed by the fact that God had blessed his journey and allowed him to meet Isaac's bride-to-be.

The servant then asked Rebekah about her family and about the possibility of staying overnight in their home. She told him to follow her, and shortly after, he met Rebekah's family and began to share with them his identity and the purpose of his mission.

As the servant recounted the story of his journey, he magnified his master's greatness (Gen. 24:35). He also explained the love that Abraham had for his son and the importance of Abraham having a daughter-in-law from his own family. It was at this same time that the servant spoke to Rebekah's father and brother about the possibility of her going home with him to become Isaac's bride.

I can only imagine that something was beginning to stir in Rebekah's heart as the servant continued to share significant details about Isaac and the goodness of his father, Abraham. Even at that moment, she may have found herself longing to go with the servant to Abraham's house to meet Isaac face to face.

As the time approached for Rebekah to say goodbye to her family, her brother and mother asked Abraham's servant if she could stay with them for at least another ten days. When the servant requested that he be allowed to return to his master with Rebekah that very day, they said, "'Let's call the girl and ask her about it.' So they called Rebekah and asked her, 'Will you go with this man?' 'I will go,' she said" (Gen. 24:57-58).

What Rebekah had heard from Abraham's servant had empowered her to leave her family and everything that had been familiar to her. She decided to follow the servant back to Abraham's house in order to meet her future husband for the very first time. The servant became both a guide and a friend to Rebekah as he encouraged her to keep her heart and mind focused on the *handsome* Isaac so she would have the strength to complete the long journey.

One day, as Rebekah was finally about to arrive at Abraham's home, she suddenly spotted Isaac walking in a nearby field. She was able to recognize him because of what she had been told about him. Rebekah dismounted from her camel, and the servant introduced her to Isaac. Isaac was captivated by her beauty and was delighted that she was the one his father had provided for him. Isaac took Rebekah into his mother's tent, and she became his wife (Gen. 24:67).

It's a mysterious, yet fascinating story. However, the spiritual implications of this story are absolutely heartwarming. Think about it—as Abraham sent his servant into a far-away country to find a bride for his son, so the Father has sent the Holy Spirit into the earth to find a bride for His Son.

The Holy Spirit brings gifts from the Father's house to woo us and awaken our hearts to the goodness of the Father. As the Holy Spirit begins to reveal to us the beauty of the Son, we find ourselves falling more and more in love with Him.

We become eager to follow the Holy Spirit on a journey through this life to a place we've never been in order to meet Someone we've never seen. Just imagine—a time is coming when we will see our Bridegroom face to face. He is going to find us radiantly beautiful, and His heart is going to be completely satisfied with us forever!

BOAZ AND RUTH

One of the clearest illustrations of the eternal romance between Christ and His bride is found in the book of Ruth. The story of Boaz and Ruth is a beautiful prophetic picture of the heavenly Father embracing people outside the nation of Israel and choosing them to be married to His Son.

As the story develops, we discover that Ruth was the Moabite daughter-in-law of a woman by the name of Naomi, who years earlier had left her Jewish homeland, along with her husband and two sons, to escape the devastating effects of a famine. The four of them eventually settled in the country of Moab, and later the two sons married Moabite women.

According to the book of Ruth, Naomi's husband suddenly died, and some time later her two sons became sick and died as well (Ruth 1:3-5). Naomi was left alone with her two daughters-in-law in a foreign country. Somehow Naomi heard that the famine had ended in Judah, so she decided to return to her homeland to try to find a relative who would take care of her. One of her daughters-in-law chose to stay in the land of Moab, but Ruth chose to return with Naomi to the land of her people.

17

The two women eventually made their way back to Naomi's homeland with nothing, and Ruth was forced to go to work in the fields, gleaning the grain left over by the harvesters. In those days, this was God's way of providing for the needy (Deut. 24:21-22).

One day while Ruth was working in the fields, Boaz, the owner of the land, noticed her. He had heard reports about a young woman who had been working extremely hard to provide for Naomi. After Boaz introduced himself to Ruth, he offered his blessing and protection to her. It was at this point that he appeared to take on the role of a father figure in the life of Ruth.

Notice the language Boaz used in addressing her: *"My daughter*, listen to me. Don't go and glean in another field and don't go away from here. Stay here with my servant girls. Watch the field where the men are harvesting, and follow along after the girls. I have told the men not to touch you. And whenever you are thirsty, go and get a drink from the water jars the men have filled" (Ruth 2:8-9, italics added).

Boaz also made sure that Ruth was given more grain than she was able to collect on her own. Later that evening, when Ruth returned home, she told Naomi all about Boaz and everything that had transpired that day. Naomi remembered that Boaz was related to her. According to the law, Boaz would have the right as a "kinsman-redeemer" to claim Naomi and Ruth as members of his household, since their husbands were no longer living.

So Naomi devised a plan and later said to Ruth, "Is not Boaz, with whose servant girls you have been, a kinsman of ours? Tonight he will be winnowing barley on the threshing floor. Wash and perfume yourself, and put on your best clothes. Then go down to the threshing floor, but don't let him know you are there until he has finished eating and drinking. When he lies down, note the place where he is lying. Then go and uncover his feet and lie down. He will tell you what to do" (Ruth 3:2-4).

Ruth obeyed her mother-in-law by doing as she was instructed. In the middle of the night, Boaz woke up and discovered Ruth lying at his feet. While he was recovering from the initial shock, she proceeded to tell him that she was related to him.

Although Boaz was fully aware of the situation, his encounter with Ruth that night instilled an even deeper desire in his heart to be the kinsman-redeemer that Naomi and Ruth needed. But he also remembered that there was someone else who lived nearby who was more closely related to them. Boaz was obligated by law to give the man an opportunity to care for the two women, but the man didn't want to take any responsibility for them. So Boaz, as a kinsman-redeemer, took Naomi and Ruth under his wing.

Boaz married Ruth, and God blessed them with a son who they named Obed. He became the grandfather of King David, and the lineage of the Messiah was forever established.

Now, there are several things about this story that deeply move me. Boaz first postured himself before Ruth as a father. This is what gave her the security she needed as a young widow living in a foreign country. The more she submitted to his care and rested in his love, the more this aspect of their relationship was established.

But over time, it became obvious that there was more in the heart of Boaz than simply wanting to be a father figure to Ruth. Boaz became enamored by her beauty and character. And then, on that one eventful night, as she lay at his feet, her perfume overwhelmed him. He found himself wanting to be more than just a father to Ruth. In the purest of ways, he wanted to know her as a husband knows his wife. And so he redeemed her for himself and took her to be his bride.

For us, the life of Boaz becomes a wonderful, earthly example of the love that God has for us as He makes Himself known to us as both a Father and a Bridegroom. First of all, God loves us as a Father to firmly establish us in our core identity as His children. This is what initially gives us the love and security that we need as human beings.

God then reveals Himself to us as our Bridegroom in order to awaken holy, passionate feelings in us that can only be experienced as we begin to understand His deepest affections for us. To think that the heart of God is overcome by the perfume of our lives—it's beyond our comprehension. Yet, it's the revelation of Jesus as our Bridegroom that ultimately melts our hearts and creates in us a burning desire for Him that can never be extinguished.

THE SONG OF SOLOMON

No study of the bridal theme would be complete without at least looking briefly at the poetic symbolism found in the Song of Solomon. Although there are a number of illustrations in the Bible that enhance our understanding of the bridal perspective concerning the kingdom of God, nothing comes close to the beauty and imagery of the love story that has come to be called the Song of Solomon.

There's no question that this deeply romantic story is about King Solomon's love for a beautiful, young Shulamite woman, yet Jewish rabbis have believed for hundreds of years that the Song of Solomon is an unparalleled depiction of God's infinite love for Israel. Over the centuries, Bible scholars have also studied the book from an allegorical perspective and viewed the song as a breathtaking prophetic portrait of Christ's love for His bride.

While it is impossible at this point to go into much detail concerning the vast amount of wealth contained in the song, it is imperative we understand that the Holy Spirit gave us this incredible book as a gift in order for us to know and feel the pure, passionate affections that the Lord has for us.[1]

It is in this eight-chapter love song that the Holy Spirit seeks to unveil to us the breathtaking personality of the Son of God and the pleasure that can be experienced in being loved by Him. This is what will capture our hearts in a fresh way and stir us to new depths of passion for Him.

We see this acted out in the life of the young Shulamite maiden. As her heart was awakened to the reality of her king's passion for her, she couldn't help crying out, "Let him kiss me with the kisses of his mouth—for your love is more delightful than wine" (Song of Sol. 1:2). She wanted more than just the casual kiss on the cheek from a friend or relative. Her heart longed for a deeper intimacy with the king. She had come to realize that the love and affections of the king were better than anything the wine of this world had to offer her.

The Shulamite's encounters with the king are meant to vividly illustrate what can take place in each of us as our hearts are melted by the beauty of our King and His extravagant feelings for us. Even now, the Holy Spirit wants to create in us a deeper hunger for intimacy with the Son of God. He longs for us to experience "the kisses of the King's mouth" to empower us to love Jesus more than ever before.

But what is meant by "the kisses of his mouth"? The phrase is poetic symbolism and refers to the Scriptures themselves. It is God affirming His love for us through the language of the Bible. The revelation of the Lord's tender affections for us is what heals our damaged emotions and rejuvenates our lives. It is a kiss unlike any other, yet it is something for which our hearts were made. It is the *one* thing in life we were truly meant to enjoy.

Another thing that really stands out in the Song of Solomon is the fact that the Lord delights in us even in our brokenness and weakness. God isn't cold, rigid, and demanding, as many think He is. In reality, just the opposite is true. He can't get enough of us. Song of Solomon 4:9 tells us that He is ravished by us! His heart is overcome with emotion because of who He has made us to be for Himself.

God doesn't just tolerate us. He enjoys us even though we may still be immature in some ways. *His estimation of our lives comes from His immeasurable love for us and is not a result of any achievement on our part.* Although we may not like ourselves or may not feel we can ultimately measure up to what is expected of us, the Lord is fascinated by us and yearns for us to live out of this reality.

He does not accuse us of our failures or condemn us for our immaturity. Instead, He continually seeks to affirm us in His love, to awaken confidence in us so that we will grow and mature.

This truth is graphically reinforced for us in Song of Solomon 4:7, when the king says to the young Shulamite, "All beautiful you are, my darling; there is no flaw in you." Although the bride hadn't come to a place where her love had fully blossomed, the bridegroom affirmed her in such a way that suggested her love for him was fully mature.

Was the king blinded by love? Of course not! In reality, he was speaking to her destiny. He was seeing the end from the beginning. He was relating to her in light of what his loving commitment would one day produce in her.

Far too many of us are still trapped by our past failures. We are constantly reminding ourselves of our short-comings, and we have even come to believe that God is against us, accusing and condemning us. We have attributed to God what is only true of Satan, who is the accuser of the brethren and the one who condemns.

Our Bridegroom is our best Friend. He is always affirming us in His love and encouraging us to look to the future. He sees the sincerity of our hearts and treats us accordingly. He never accuses or condemns us. He is constantly speaking over us, calling forth our destiny. He knows what His lavish commitment to us will one day produce because His desire has always been to bring us to a place of mature love.

This is why it is essential for us to stand in the truth of His assessment of our lives. We need to pray for the grace to receive His tender affirmations concerning us. Deep down inside, we have always wanted to be loved like this. It's time we realize that the passionate love shared between the king and the Shulamite is only a dim reflection of the kind of love that burns in the heart of Jesus for us, His bride.

Together, we have looked at some amazing stories that have highlighted the bridal theme of Scripture. I would encourage you, in your own quiet time, to meditate on these passages. I believe the Holy Spirit wants to open your heart and mind even more to these wonderful truths so you'll be transformed by the beauty of what you discover.

CLOSING PRAYER

Father, in the Name of Jesus, I thank You for giving me Your Son. Jesus, I pray that You would continue to draw me deeper into the beauty of who You are. I want to know You as my Bridegroom. May the revelation of Your passion for me warm my heart like never before. Amen.

Chapter Three

THE FATHER
OF THE BRIDE

The romance between Adam and Eve was a match made in heaven. They truly had been made for each other. Their covenant love was meant to last through the ages, with the two of them living together happily ever after. But something sinister took place shortly after their honeymoon. The heart of the young bride was seduced by another, and what started out as the perfect love story became the greatest human tragedy of all time.

But something almost as tragic took place as well. When the serpent approached Eve with his titillating proposal, the stage was set for Adam to intervene. You would've expected him to come running to the aid of his wife, crushing the serpent's head, and putting an end to the heinous seduction of evil. Yet when Adam was confronted with the horror of what was taking place, he wilted under the pressure.

Have you ever wondered what Adam was doing while his wife was being propositioned? He was right there with her, watching her contemplate spiritual suicide. "When the woman saw that the fruit of the tree was good for food and pleasing to the eye, and also desirable for gaining wisdom, she took some and ate. She also gave some to her husband, who was with her, and he ate it" (Gen. 3:6).

Did you catch it? The text says, "She also gave some to her husband who was *with her*." As naturally strong as Adam probably was, when it came time for him to protect his woman, he just stood there. He didn't do what any true, red-blooded husband should do; he didn't defend and look after the wife God gave him.

At that moment, Adam turned his back on the two great loves of his life—God and his wife. What followed changed human history. The first couple had drunk from the fountain of all love; they had lived in unbroken communion with the most breathtaking, beautiful, and intoxicating source of life and passion in the universe.

Yet, in one swift moment in time, Adam and Eve ran and hid from the One who had made them for Himself. The pure pleasure and intimacy they had enjoyed with the Lord were gone. Paradise appeared to have been lost.

However, there would be One who would stop at nothing when the loves of His life were taken from Him. Another Adam would invade planet earth and fight for His beloved. He would utterly defeat the Great Seducer of the human race. He would also keep a promise He had made before time began, and He would love a woman—a bride— who had been given to Him by His Father.

There is even a hint of this climactic event found in Genesis 3:15. God said to the serpent, "And I will put enmity between you and the woman, and between your seed and her Seed; He shall bruise your head, and you shall bruise His heel" (NKJV).

Please notice the phrase "her Seed" and the fact that the word Seed is capitalized. Because a woman doesn't have seed, what is implied in the text is that the Seed of Eve is actually referring to Christ. Verse 15 is really a prophecy foreshadowing the eventual death of Jesus and the fact that one day He would pay the ultimate "bride price."

The Godhead was not caught off guard by the betrayal of the first couple. Before the beginning of time, it had been *predetermined* that the eternal Son of God would become a man, step onto the stage of life, woo His beloved, win her hand, and make her His queen.

But how would all of this play out in the arena of human experience? We are given a clue in Galatians 3. In the last part of verse 8, we are told that all the nations of the world would be blessed through a man by the name of Abraham. Then in verse 16 of the same chapter, we read these words: "Now to Abraham and his Seed were the promises made. He does not say, 'And to seeds,' as of many, but as of one, 'And to your Seed,' who is Christ" (NKJV).

While the language of these verses may not mean much to us initially, the words carry us back in time to a series of events that also changed human history forever. Approximately five hundred years after the Flood, God spoke to a man by the name of Abram (who would later become known as Abraham) and called him to a covenant of love. Abram was told to leave his country and go to a land that God would show him. God said He would bless him and make him into a great nation. The Lord also promised Abram that all the peoples of the earth would be blessed through him (Gen. 12:1-7).

So God brought Abram to a land called Canaan and approached him in a way he could understand—He entered into a blood covenant with him. Because covenant was something familiar to those living in that time period,

Abram understood, to some degree, the significance of what was taking place.

THE MEANING OF COVENANT

The covenant ceremony is described for us in Genesis 15:

> After these things the word of the LORD came to Abram in a vision, saying, "Do not be afraid, Abram. I am your shield, your exceedingly great reward" … So he said to him, "Bring Me a three-year-old heifer, a three-year-old female goat, a three-year-old ram, a turtledove, and a young pigeon." Then he brought all these to Him and cut them in two, down the middle, and placed each piece opposite each other; but he did not cut the birds in two. And when the vultures came down on the carcasses, Abram drove them away. Now when the sun was going down, a deep sleep fell upon Abram; and behold, horror and great darkness fell upon him. Then He said to Abram: "Know certainly that your descendants will be strangers in a land that is not theirs, and will serve them, and they will afflict them four hundred years. And also the nation whom they serve I will judge; afterward they shall come out with great possessions. Now as for you, you shall go to your fathers in peace; you shall be buried at a good old age. But in the fourth generation they shall return here, for the iniquity of the Amorites is not yet

complete." And it came to pass, when the sun went down and it was dark, that behold, there was a smoking oven and a burning torch that passed between those pieces. On the same day the LORD made a covenant with Abram, saying: "To your descendants I have given this land, from the river of Egypt to the great river, the River Euphrates" (Gen. 15:1, 9-18, NKJV).

It's significant that the first promise God made to Abram after initiating the covenant ceremony was "I am your shield, your exceedingly great reward." With this one statement, God was offering Himself completely to Abram. In essence, the Lord was saying, "I will always be here for you. I will protect and defend you. Your struggles will be My struggles. All that I am I give to you. I will be whatever you need Me to be at any given moment in time."

What a promise! On the surface, it sounds too good to be true. To think that God would be *everything* to this man is really beyond comprehension. And yet, when we understand the nature of covenant, we won't be surprised by the great lengths to which God went in order to reveal Himself to Abram.

You see, a covenant was a binding agreement between two parties. But, in reality, it was so much more than just a mere contract. The Old Testament Hebrew word for covenant literally means "to cut" or "to cut in pieces." Similarly, the New Testament Greek word for covenant means "to cut a covenant." By definition then, the "cutting of a covenant" was an agreement between two parties, sealed by the shedding of blood.

A blood covenant was the most endearing and enduring of all contracts. It was also the most sacred and solemn thing into which two parties could enter. A covenant bound the participants together. It was not a casual commitment at all. When a person entered into covenant with someone, he promised to give his life, his love, and everything that was a part of him. Involved in this covenant were the very issues of life and death.

This is the reason the implications of what was being offered to Abram were staggering. The covenant that Abram was invited to embrace was actually a bond in blood, executed by the sovereign authority of the Godhead. Think of it—God chose to enter into a special relationship with Abram in which He promised to be everything to him. God also told Abram that He would give him all the land of Canaan and that his descendants would be as great in number as the stars of heaven.

Although these promises were absolutely mind-boggling to Abram, he chose to believe what God had spoken to him (Gen. 15:6). However, there was just one question that Abram needed to have answered. It's recorded for us in verse 8 of the same chapter: "O Sovereign Lord, how can I know that I will gain possession of it?" In light of everything that was unfolding at that moment in Abram's life, his question was a very significant one.

THE MAKING OF COVENANT

God responded to Abram's question with some very specific instructions that he would clearly understand. According to Genesis 15:9, God said, "Bring me a heifer, a goat and a ram, each three years old, along with a dove and a young pigeon." Abram quickly gathered up the animals and then cut the heifer, goat, and ram down the middle and laid the halves opposite each other (Gen. 15:10).

When God instructed Abram to split the animals down the middle and divide the halves, he knew what God intended to do because this was not an uncommon practice in his day. Abram understood that God was cutting a covenant with him. He knew he could expect God's promises to be fulfilled because of what the covenant guaranteed him.

Because of its serious nature, a blood covenant was actually referred to as a "walk of death." As the pieces of the dismembered animals were laid opposite each other, half on one side and half on the other with a space left in the middle, the participants in the covenant ceremony walked a figure-eight pattern between the cut pieces. As they met in the middle of the pieces, they pronounced all the blessings and conditions of the covenant, as well as the curses for breaking it.

For the covenant participants, this walk of death symbolized a total commitment to each other. It meant that each individual would no longer live for himself but, instead, for his covenant partner. It was a death to all independent living.

This covenant bond also required the parties involved to exchange all their assets, obligations, and liabilities with each other. There was even an exchange of enemies. For example, if you had been living in that day and you chose to cut covenant with someone, all your liabilities would be his responsibility if you were unable to meet your obligations. However, the same would be true if he were in need, since all your assets would be at his disposal. Furthermore, all your enemies would be declared your partner's enemies, and he would have to vow to fight them on your behalf. You, in turn, would do the same for your covenant partner.

In cutting covenant with Abram, God was promising to make this kind of exchange with him. The Lord would take all of Abram's obligations and liabilities upon Himself. He also promised to declare all of Abram's enemies His enemies. But this exchange also meant that Abram would have to walk in covenant with God and that all his possessions would belong to the Lord. There was only one problem. How could Abram truly enter into covenant with Almighty God? What could he offer the Lord anyway? Besides, God had no liabilities, and there were certainly no enemies that posed any threat to Him.

THE MOTIVATION FOR COVENANT

Normally, when two parties entered into a covenant agreement, they each walked between the pieces of the dead animals. However, this was not the case with Abram. God caused a deep sleep to come upon him (Gen. 15:12). The Septuagint, which is the Greek translation of the Old Testament, translated the Hebrew word "tardemah" as *ecstasy*, rather than *deep sleep*. This is quite significant because the use of this word seems to reinforce the idea that Abram was in a trance-like state, having a profound prophetic experience.

It appears that Abram caught a glimpse of something so *awesome* and *profound* that he was enraptured by what he saw and experienced! I believe, in part, this is what Jesus may have been referring to when He said, "Your father Abraham rejoiced at the thought of seeing my day; he saw it and was glad" (John 8:56).

Why are all these details so important for us to grasp? They're significant because of what immediately followed. While Abram was under the influence of this powerful, prophetic vision, God told him that his descendants would be in bondage in a strange country for four hundred years. But the Lord also promised that one day they would be delivered with great wealth.

Then Abram saw what appeared to be "a smoking oven and a burning torch that passed between those pieces" (Gen. 15:17, NKJV). Who or what was it that moved between the pieces of the dead animals on Abram's behalf? In the book of Revelation, John described in vivid detail a vision he had seen of Jesus: "His head and hair were white like wool, as white as snow, and His eyes like a flame of fire [burning torch]; His feet were like fine brass, as if refined in a furnace [a smoking oven]" (Rev. 1:14-15, NKJV, emphasis added).

It was the Son of God, in His pre-incarnate glory, who walked between the pieces on Abram's behalf. Before time began, the Son had made a promise to His Father. What was that promise? The Son had agreed to take Abram's place. He would walk the walk of death for Abram and his descendants. He would come as the fulfillment of the covenant.

The death of the animals sacrificed by Abram was symbolic of the supreme sacrifice that would be made one day on behalf of mankind. Christ Himself would come as the Lamb of God to take away the sin of the world. He would free us from being held captive by the lies of the evil one. The blood of Jesus would wash away our shame forever.

But why would Christ do such a thing? What was His motivation for going to such great lengths to redeem humanity for Himself? Remember, the Son of God had been promised a bride. It now is apparent that the Father had selected a bride for His Son from Abram's seed. In the eternal plan of the Godhead, Abram had been chosen to be the "father of the bride." The Son of God had agreed to pay the "ultimate bride price" by offering Himself in death in order to purchase the wife who had been chosen for Him.

To fully grasp the significance of Christ's sacrifice, we need to realize that in the Jewish culture brides were purchased. A "bride price" had to be paid to the father of the prospective bride. This tradition was not demeaning for women of that period. In fact, just the opposite was true. One of the primary reasons a bride price was paid was to show how much the bridegroom loved and valued his future wife. This makes the language of 1 Peter 1:18-19 even more meaningful to us: "For you know that it was not with perishable things such as silver or gold that you were redeemed [bought, purchased] ... but with the precious blood of Christ, a lamb without blemish or defect" (emphasis added).

Jesus valued the love and affection of His bride so much that to Him silver and gold weren't good enough for her. He chose, instead, to spill His own blood in order to win her hand in marriage. He would walk the "walk of death" so that He could live with her and enjoy her forever.

But that's not the end of the story. Before God finished making covenant with Abram, He changed his name to Abraham. However, it was much more than just a mere name change. Bob Phillips, in his book titled, *Covenant: Its Blessings, Its Curses*, strongly suggests that according to Jewish tradition, the letters "ah" in the Hebrew language are used to depict the expulsion of God's breath. He writes, "It is a part of the unspoken name of 'Yahweh.' In changing Abram's name to Abraham, God breathed His own life into him, making an exchange of His name with that of Abraham's."[1]

In doing so, the Lord was promising not only to identify Himself with Abraham as a part of His own family, but He was pointing to a time in the future when, as a Bridegroom, He would enter His bride by His Spirit.

MADE FOR COVENANT LOVE

The Lord's desire has always been to have a people who would be a "treasured possession" to Him (Exod. 19:5). He has forever longed to have a people for Himself so He could be one with them. All the covenants in the Bible from Adam to Jesus find their fulfillment in the Father's desire to have a bride for His Son with whom He could be intimate. This is "the mystery that has been kept hidden for ages and generations, but is now disclosed to the saints. To them God has chosen to make known among the Gentiles the glorious riches of this mystery, which is *Christ in you*, the hope of glory" (Col. 1:26-27, italics added).

Think about it! The Lord loved us so much that all His actions portrayed in the pages of the Bible are meant to convey His deepest feelings for us and His desire to be our Lover and best Friend. He has further expressed the passion of His heart in the incredible words found in 1 Corinthians 11:24: "This is My body which is broken for you" (NKJV).

35

For many of you this story may sound like something right out of a Hollywood movie. But the truth is—it's so much better than that! However, if this storyline were a part of a Hollywood script, I believe it would read something like this:

> Once up a time there was a beautiful maiden … She might be the daughter of a king or a common servant girl, but we know she is a princess at heart. She is young with a youth that seems eternal … But this lovely maiden is unattainable, the prisoner of an evil power who holds her captive in a dark tower. Only a champion may win her; only the most valiant, daring, and brave warrior has a chance of setting her free. Against all hope he comes; with cunning and raw courage he lays siege to the tower and the sinister one who holds her. Much blood is shed on both sides; three times the knight is thrown back, but three times he rises again. Eventually the sorcerer is defeated, the dragon falls, the giant is slain. The maiden is his; through his valor he has won her heart.[2]

CLOSING PRAYER

Father, in the Name of Jesus, open my heart and mind to understand the fullness of the covenant relationship I have with You. Awaken my heart to Your affections. Release the passion of Your love within me. Help me to see myself as the bride of Christ. Amen.

Chapter Four

A SACRED MARRIAGE PROPOSAL

The word of the Lord came to me: "Son of man, confront Jerusalem with her detestable practices and say, 'This is what the Sovereign Lord says to Jerusalem: Your ancestry and birth were in the land of the Canaanites; your father was an Amorite and your mother a Hittite. On the day you were born your cord was not cut, nor were you washed with water to make you clean, nor were you rubbed with salt or wrapped in cloths. No one looked on you with pity or had compassion enough to do any of these things for you. Rather, you were thrown out into the open field, for on the day you were born you were despised. Then I passed by and saw you kicking about in your blood, and as you lay there in your blood I said to you, "Live!" I made you grow like a plant of the field. You grew up and developed and became the most beautiful of jewels'" (Ezek. 16:1-7).

ADOPTING A NATION

These verses are a part of one of the most picturesque passages found in the Bible. The language is intriguing, as it paints for the reader verbal pictures of Israel's beginning as a nation. With one broad stroke of the brush, the prophet Ezekiel captures the imagination as he portrays the passion and drama of God loving a people and choosing them for Himself.

Poetic imagery is initially used by Ezekiel to depict the utter devastation and hopelessness in which the Hebrew people were wallowing when the Lord first revealed Himself to them. The plight of these poor slaves is compared to a newborn baby girl who had been abandoned by her parents. Her mother had given birth to her in an open field and then left her to die, exposed to the elements. Her father wanted nothing to do with her. To make matters worse, neither one of her parents had the decency to cut her navel cord and wash the afterbirth from her tiny, frail body.

With graphic, gut-wrenching language, the prophet brings us face to face with the overwhelming sense of abandonment and rejection Abraham's offspring felt as they found themselves enslaved by the nation of Egypt. What must be understood is that from the time God said to Abraham, "I will establish my covenant as an everlasting covenant between me and you and your descendants after you for the generations to come, to be your God and the God of your descendants after you" (Gen. 17:7), to the time He made Himself known to the children of Israel, 430 long years had come and gone.

Yet the Lord's original intention for the Hebrew people never changed. The beauty and emotion conveyed in the words penned by Ezekiel only further illustrate this for us:

38

"Then I passed by and saw you kicking about in your blood, and as you lay there in your blood I said to you, 'Live!' I made you grow like a plant of the field. You grew up and developed and became the most beautiful of jewels" (Ezek. 16:6-7).

The colorful language of verses 6 and 7 truly captures the essence of what the Lord first said to Moses in Exodus 6:5-8:

> Moreover, I have heard the groaning of the Israelites, whom the Egyptians are enslaving, and I have remembered my covenant. Therefore, say to the Israelites: "I am the Lord, and I will bring you out from under the yoke of the Egyptians. I will free you from being slaves to them, and I will redeem you with an outstretched arm and with mighty acts of judgment. I will take you as my own people, and I will be your God. Then you will know that I am the Lord your God, who brought you out from under the yoke of the Egyptians. And I will bring you to the land I swore … to give to Abraham, to Isaac and to Jacob. I will give it to you as a possession. I am the Lord."

Although these two passages may appear to be quite different because of the wording that's used, they're actually describing the same events. Hundreds of years after Israel's departure from Egypt, Ezekiel, through the art of storytelling, was able to vividly portray the Lord's love for His children in a way not found in the Exodus account.

God deliberately used the language of Ezekiel 16:6-7 to communicate His tender affections for Israel when the nation was first born and to express His profound feelings for them as their Father. What these verses beautifully articulate are the deeply passionate words of a father to a child.

Everything God did in delivering His children from Egypt was meant to demonstrate His parental, take-charge attitude. From the outset, the Lord wanted Israel to understand His heart so they wouldn't misinterpret what He was going to allow to happen to the Egyptians and end up being afraid of Him.

From their first day of slavery in Egypt to the moment they were set free, the Hebrew people had only known the haunting fear of their "masters" and the gods they had been forced to serve. Yet when the Lord delivered them from the tyranny of the Egyptians, the people still clung to their idols. They were utterly clueless about His affections for them.

The Lord desired that His children would begin to comprehend His intentions and would learn to live in such *awe* of Him that they wouldn't have any problems trusting Him, regardless of what they had to face. Nothing He had *allowed* was meant to scare them. It wasn't about that at all! From the very first moment He began revealing Himself to them, all He had ever wanted was their love and devotion.

This is why the Lord had instructed Moses earlier to tell the people "I AM has sent me to you" (Exod. 3:14). When He referred to Himself as I AM, He was saying to His children, "I AM whatever you need Me to be at any given moment in time. I AM your Everlasting Father. I AM your Provider. I AM the One who cares for you. Whenever you have a need, there I AM."

40

The nature of the language of verse 14 and what was being promised to the children of Israel may remind us of something the Lord once said to Abraham in Genesis 17:1: "I am God Almighty; walk before me and be blameless." The phrase *Almighty God* means "nurse" or "all-sufficient One." As the ultimate *Parent*, the Lord was assuring not only Abraham but also his descendants that He would nurse them and care for them as One who was more than capable of meeting their every need.

Having delivered the children of Israel from the clutches of Egypt, the Lord nurtured the fledgling nation with mineral spring water, manna hot cakes, and filet of quail. His loving care for them was intended to vividly illustrate His fatherly affections for them. He wanted to wean them off the things of Egypt and, at the same time, nurse them with His love.

But the people still didn't get it. They didn't grasp the significance of the name by which He had revealed Himself. From the Red Sea to Mount Sinai, they murmured against Him and continually questioned His intentions. By the time they reached the Wilderness of Sinai, the people were weary of the journey and thoroughly confused about their destiny. It was all too apparent that they really didn't know the One who had chosen them. So the Lord took the opportunity to introduce Himself again to Israel. And what an introduction it was!

CHOOSING A WIFE

God initially sought to reveal Himself to the children of Israel as their caring, loving Father. This should have given them the security they needed and enabled them to rest in

41

His love. However, the revelation of the Father's heart was also intended to prepare the children of Israel for their ultimate destiny. Just as the love of a father prepares a young woman for her wedding day, the love of the Father was meant to prepare Israel for her wedding day.

But in order for God to deepen Israel's understanding of His ultimate intention, as well as demonstrate His pure, passionate love for her, He made a *proposal* to her that was out of this world. Using beautiful, poetic language, He instructed Moses to tell her, "You yourselves have seen what I did to Egypt, and how I carried you on eagles' wings and brought you to myself. Now if you obey me fully and keep my *covenant*, then out of all nations you will be my *treasured possession*" (Exod. 19:4-5, italics added).

According to Jewish tradition, the covenant God initiated with His people at Mount Sinai was really a covenant of marriage. In fact, rabbis have believed for centuries that the Jewish wedding ceremony was not only a re-enactment of what happened at Sinai, but it also reflected the primary features of God's covenant with Israel.

This truth is reinforced by the stunning symbolism of Ezekiel 16. In this picturesque passage, the Lord was able to beautifully illustrate in one verse His passionate encounter with Israel at Sinai and the marriage proposal He made to her. "Later I passed by, and when I looked at you and saw that you were old enough for love, I spread the corner of my garment over you and covered your nakedness. I gave you my solemn oath and entered into a covenant with you, declares the Sovereign Lord, and you became mine" (Ezek. 16:8).

Remember, the Bible likens God to a Bridegroom and Israel to His wife (Isa. 54:5-6; 62:5). The Lord said to Jeremiah, "The time is coming ... when I will make a new covenant with the house of Israel and with the house of Judah. It will not be like the covenant I made with their forefathers when I took them by the hand to lead them out of Egypt, because they broke my covenant, though I was a husband to them" (Jer. 31:31-32). Furthermore, Hellenistic Judaism interpreted the Song of Solomon as an allegory portraying the love relationship between God and Israel, His wife.

Throughout the Old Testament, the Lord used breath-taking, bridal language to convey His burning desire for His people and to reveal His heart to them as their Bridegroom. But it was the bridal imagery of Exodus 19-20 that initially awakened Israel to her ultimate destiny as God's wife. This is highlighted for us in several significant ways.*

THE BETROTHAL

An ancient Jewish wedding consisted of two main parts, beginning with a betrothal. A marriage contract (*ketubah*) detailing the terms and obligations of the union was read to the bride before she was asked to make her final commitment to the bridegroom. The rabbis point out that this act was first depicted in Scripture when the Lord declared to Israel on Sinai, "Now if you obey me fully and keep my covenant, then out of all nations you will be my treasured possession. Although the whole earth is mine, you will be for me a kingdom of priests and a holy nation" (Exod. 19:5-6).

The following verse explains that "Moses went back and summoned the elders of the people and set before them all the words the Lord had commanded him to speak" (Exod. 19:7). Just as a *ketubah* set forth the conditions and expectations for a marriage, the contract offered to Israel on Sinai detailed the divine conditions stipulated by the Lord.

THE ACT OF CONSECRATION

In early rabbinic literature, the first part of the marriage ceremony, which contractually set the couple aside in betrothal, was known as an act of "sanctification" or "consecration" (*kiddushin*). The basic meaning behind the term *kiddushin* is "to be set apart" or "to be holy." The rabbis have long pointed to this concept of sanctification as central to the covenant God made with Israel on Sinai. This is why the Lord said to Moses, "Go to the people and consecrate them today and tomorrow" (Exod. 19:10). The people were to be sanctified and separated to the Lord as a chaste virgin in order to be ready for their marriage to Him. Israel's calling was to be a "holy nation" (Exod. 19:6).

THE PERIOD OF PREPARATION

Because marriage was viewed by the Jewish community as a lifelong covenant between two people, a betrothal period was set aside for preparation. A wedding was never to be a spur-of-the-moment event. One was expected to prepare for marriage by giving it serious consideration and forethought. Only later was the relationship fully consummated.

According to Exodus 19:12-15, Israel was also given a period of time to prepare herself to receive the covenant. Moses first instructed the people to wash their clothes. This act of purification later came to symbolize the process every bride had to go through to prepare for her wedding.

In this passage, husbands were even told not to have sexual relations with their wives during the entire preparation process. This may have been required to illustrate the importance of being separated and consecrated to the Lord in order to experience true intimacy with Him.

The people were also warned not to approach Mount Sinai until the preparation period was complete. It wasn't that the Lord was distant and unapproachable or that He was trying to make things as difficult as possible for His future wife. Rather, He wanted her to understand the serious nature of the covenant into which she was about to enter. His *transcendent beauty* and *splendor* were such that Israel needed to prepare for her union with Him.

THE COVENANT PLEDGE

According to Jewish culture, the concept of covenant taught couples that in marriage one must be a person of one's word. Just as Israel pledged publicly at Sinai her full agreement to the terms of the covenant, marriage also required no less a response on the part of each individual. To the Jew, one's word was considered equal to one's promise. When Israel said, "We will do everything the Lord has said" (Exod. 19:8), she was making a promise to uphold her end of the covenant requirements, as well as vowing to remain forever faithful to her Husband.

THE COMING OF THE BRIDEGROOM

In the Jewish wedding ceremony, the bridegroom would be the first to come to the bridal canopy (*huppah*) and wait for the coming of his bride. The groom would be accompanied by two attendants. The couple would stand together under the *huppah* throughout the service. The rabbis have taught that this tradition began when the Lord first descended upon Mount Sinai in fire and waited for the people to be brought out of the camp to meet with Him (Exod. 19:16-18). In addition, some rabbis have suggested that when the Lord came to Sinai for His extravagant marriage to Israel, He was accompanied by two attendants. In this case, the two attendants were the two tablets of stone upon which the Ten Commandments were written.

THE PROCESSION BY FIRE

For generations, it was the practice in the Jewish community for the bridegroom and bride to make their way to the bridal canopy accompanied by attendants carrying candles or lamps. This is wonderfully depicted in the movie *Fiddler on the Roof.* Also, the parable of the ten virgins in Matthew 25 is a biblical account of a wedding that included the use of lamps and possibly even torches.

Again, some rabbis point to Sinai as the origin of such a practice. On the day of the covenant ceremony between the Lord and Israel, the people heard the thunder and saw the lightning and smoke (Exod. 19:16; 20:18). In these verses, the Hebrew term for lightning (*lappidim*) is the same word that is often translated "torches." Just as a Jewish bride and groom were accompanied by fire (candles, lamps, and torches), Israel and the Lord were escorted by fire as well.[1]

FASCINATING SPLENDOR

The covenant ceremony between the Lord and Israel must have been spectacular. The light show alone must have been out-of-this-world! The Lord wowed His wife by putting Himself on display for her. As Moses led the people to the foot of the mountain to meet with their Bridegroom, "Mount Sinai was covered with smoke, because the Lord descended on it in fire. The smoke billowed up from it like *smoke from a furnace*, the whole mountain trembled violently" (Exod. 19:18, italics added). Notice that Moses' description of the Lord's fiery presence was very similar to the language used in Genesis 15:17 to describe the Lord as a smoking furnace (oven).

I believe the blazing fire on Mount Sinai was really a dynamic display of the Bridegroom's consuming, fiery love for His wife. It appears that the Lord was utterly determined to use the occasion to express His pure passion for Israel. But the manifestation of His holy splendor was never meant to scare her—it was meant to captivate her.

Nevertheless, Israel misinterpreted the Lord's *advances* once again. "When the people saw the thunder and lightning and heard the trumpet and saw the mountain in smoke, they trembled with fear. They stayed at a distance and said to Moses, 'Speak to us yourself and we will listen. But do not have God speak to us or we will die'" (Exod. 20:18-19).

Yet notice Moses' response to the people: "*Do not be afraid*. God has come to test you, so that the fear of God will be with you to keep you from sinning" (Exod. 20:20, italics added). It should be obvious by the first words out of Moses' mouth that God didn't want the people to be afraid of Him. Although it's true that He was testing Israel's

47

willingness to love and obey Him by offering her a proposal of marriage, the Lord never wanted a cringing, fearful subject for a wife.

The Lord wanted Israel to be so fascinated by Him that she would never give her heart to other lovers. This is why He appeared to her the way He did. He wanted her to be in *awe* of Him to such a degree that she wouldn't sin by going after the gods of other nations. This is really what Moses was implying when he told the people that the Lord was going to place His fear (awe) before them so they wouldn't sin.

Fascination is the very essence of the fear of the Lord. The *awe* and subsequent *humility* one experiences when brought face to face with the transcendent (unequaled, surpassing, matchless) splendor and beauty of God are what truly define the fear of the Lord. *Awe* can include emotion, but it's more than that. It's the sense of *wonder* that awakens one's heart to the knowledge of who God really is.

God made the human heart with an inextinguishable desire to be fascinated. This is what the Lord appealed to when He sought to woo the nation of Israel to Himself. He localized Himself on Sinai and displayed His majesty in order to powerfully demonstrate to her that, although He is holy and transcendently (supremely) different from all others, he was willing to give Himself to her. And while He is in a class all by Himself, He chose to love her and reveal Himself to her as the Holy One of Israel.

But the divine dilemma has always been—how does the Lord captivate the hearts of human beings without consuming them with His splendor? How does He just be Himself and, at the same time, not overwhelm them or even destroy them? This dilemma seems to be the motivating force behind the passionate language used by the Lord in Exodus 19:21-22.

According to Isaiah 6:2-3, the seraphim (lit. *burning ones*) can't even gaze directly at the dazzling splendor and beauty of the Lord. Imagine a beauty so intensely perfect and breathtaking that it's both overwhelming and pleasurable at the same time. The angelic hosts around the throne of God aren't crying, "holy, holy, holy" out of fear or obligation. They are caught up in the undiluted pleasure of God's presence as He continually unveils His radiant magnificence to them as Father, Son, and Holy Spirit.

Although the Lord is holy and transcendent, He is not inaccessible. While He is infinitely lofty, He is never distant and aloof. As we have seen in Israel's case, God's *fascinating splendor* would not prevent Him from drawing near in mercy to those with whom He had entered into covenant. He couldn't keep from *showing Himself off* to a nation with whom He had fallen in love!

ENDNOTE

*For a further study of this subject, read *Our Father Abraham*, by Marvin R. Wilson.

CLOSING PRAYER

Father, in the Name of Jesus, I ask You to remove the scales from my eyes so I can see You for who You really are. I don't want to blindly follow religious concepts about You that have veiled Your beauty from me. I'm tired of being scared of You. Fascinate me with Your love so that my passion for You will never be the same. Amen.

Chapter Five

COMMANDMENTS OR A MARRIAGE CONTRACT?

Centuries ago, the translators of the Septuagint made a tragic mistake when they translated the word *Torah* (the first five books of the Bible) as *Law*. On the surface, this error may not appear to be very significant. But over the years, the misunderstanding of the meaning of Torah has produced a way of thinking that has had a profound effect on how many have come to view the Old Testament and, especially, the Ten Commandments.

The Torah is more than just a system of laws. Even though Judaism mistakenly came to be known as a religion of laws, the Jews viewed the Scriptures as teaching. They believed the Torah had been given to them by God to reveal His character. The Scriptures were meant to be a road map to lead the Jewish people into the heart of God so they could know and experience Him intimately.

When God called Israel to keep His commandments, He was actually inviting her to enter into fellowship with Him. He wanted His wife to realize that the greatest form of devotion was simply walking *with* Him. "He has showed you, O man, what is good. And what does the Lord require of you? To act justly and to love mercy and to walk humbly with your God" (Mic. 6:8).

The Torah was never about outward conformity to mere rules and regulations. The Scriptures were given to Israel so she could encounter God and begin to understand His ways. The giving of the Torah on Mount Sinai was all about relationship, not about ritual. As we've already seen, what transpired between God and Israel at Sinai wasn't just about commandments; in reality, it was all about a marriage contract.

ALL ABOUT LOVE

According to Jewish tradition, what occurred at Mount Sinai was a decisive moment in Israel's history. God became *engaged* to a people. Israel accepted the new relationship and became *engaged* to God. It was a monumental event in which both were partners. God gave His word to Israel, and Israel gave her word of honor to God.

This is why the Ten Commandments begin with the words, "I am the Lord your God, who brought you out of Egypt, out of the land of slavery. You shall have no other gods before me" (Exod. 20:2-3). As Israel's Bridegroom, God could just as easily have said, "I am the Lord your Husband; I don't want you to have any other lovers except Me."

The Lord then told His wife, "You shall not make for yourself an idol in the form of anything in heaven above or on the earth beneath or in the waters below. You shall not bow down to them or worship them ..." (Exod. 20:4-5a).

It was as if the Lord was saying to His wife, "I know where you've come from and what you've given your heart to in the past. But I'm not like the gods of the Egyptians; I'm not an inanimate object. I'm not made of wood or stone. I'm transcendent beauty! Don't give your heart to pathetic idols. Don't give yourself to the *gods* that will ultimately destroy you and your children. I wholly desire your love and devotion. Give yourself to Me with all your heart."

God then said to Israel, "You shall not misuse the name of the Lord your God, for the Lord will not hold anyone guiltless who misuses his name" (Exod. 20:7). Remember, the Lord had just proposed to Israel on Mount Sinai. He had asked her to give herself to Him in holy matrimony and to take His name just as any prospective bride would take the name of her future husband. God wanted Israel to leave her past behind and find a new identity in Him. He didn't want her taking His name in vain by wearing His ring and bearing His name before the nations of the world but acting like she was not spoken for and, therefore, available to anyone.

The Lord further instructed Israel:

> Remember the Sabbath day by keeping it holy. Six days you shall labor and do all your work, but the seventh day is a Sabbath to the Lord your God. On it you shall not do any work, neither you, nor your son or daughter, nor your manservant or maidservant, nor your animals, nor the alien within your gates. For in six days the Lord made the heavens and the earth, the sea, and all that is in them, but he rested on the seventh day. Therefore the Lord blessed the Sabbath day and made it holy (Exod. 20:8-11).

The Sabbath, however, was never meant to be about the outward observance of a particular day. Neither was the Sabbath designed by God to be a religious burden to His people. This is what Jesus was referring to when He said, "The Sabbath was made for man, not man for the Sabbath" (Mark 2:27).

Although the Sabbath was observed as a day of rest, it was never intended just to be about having a day off from physical labor. At the heart of the Sabbath was God's desire for His wife to rest in the security of His love. The rest He was calling Israel to was the rest of intimacy. The Jewish people were never called just to revere a day; they were called to honor and adore the One who commanded the observance of the Sabbath day.

The Sabbath was to be a day in which the people were to celebrate the Lord and the life they would share together. Remember, God rested on the seventh day of creation. Yet He didn't rest because He was tired from all of His activities. He rested because He wanted to pause and reflect on all He had made. He wanted to celebrate His handiwork and experience the pleasure of the love of the two people He had made for Himself.

Even to this day, the Jewish people are taught to observe the Sabbath as a day for celebrating God and the life He has given them. Parents are instructed to spend quality time with their children, and married couples are even encouraged to be intimate. The Sabbath was always meant to be about resting in the security of God's love and, as a result, living life to the fullest.

A CHANGE OF THINKING

The traditional view of the Ten Commandments suggests that the first four commandments are about man's relationship to God, while the last six commandments concern man's relationship to man. While I believe there is truth in this approach to the Ten Commandments, I'm also convinced that the last six commandments have underlying bridal implications as well.

For example, when God said to His people, "Honor your father and your mother, so that you may live long in the land the Lord your God is giving you" (Exod. 20:12), I don't believe He was just referring to the respect children should have for their parents. Although it is essential for the health of a family that children lovingly honor and obey their parents, I truly think the Lord was addressing another significant issue in this commandment.

I believe the Lord was reminding Israel of the covenant He had made with her father Abraham and was challenging her to honor and respect her sacred heritage by keeping her part of the marriage contract. Because Abraham was the father of the bride, what greater way could Israel honor her father and mother than by remaining faithful to the One to whom she had been betrothed?

God further instructed Israel, "You shall not murder" (Exod. 20:13). Yet why would God command her not to commit murder when men already knew it was wrong to take the life of another human being (Gen. 4:8-11)? The Lord was trying to teach His wife about His own heart—that murder is not something He just scorns when done by others, but that it is the very opposite of who He is. Furthermore, God didn't want Israel to misinterpret the judgments against her enemies by viewing them as acts of murder.

God also wanted His wife to properly represent Him before the other nations. This was extremely important to the Lord. This is clearly illustrated for us in the life of Moses. Many Christians believe Moses was kept out of the Promised Land because of his anger (Num. 20:7-12). But Moses was not allowed to go into the land of Canaan with the nation of Israel because his anger caused him to *misrepresent* the heart of God to her.

Moses was the Lord's representative. He was to be an example to the people of God's character. The Lord didn't want Israel to think that His primary emotion is anger. He wanted her to understand that He truly is a God of love and that He fully expected His queen to reflect His heart and character in the earth.

The Lord also commanded His people, "You shall not commit adultery" (Exod. 20:14). While it should be obvious to all of us that God was calling Jewish couples to marital fidelity, I believe He also was admonishing Israel to remember that she was His wife and that He wanted her to remain faithful to Him.

God then told Israel, "You shall not steal" (Exod. 20:15). This commandment is closely related to the tenth commandment in which the Lord further said, "You shall not covet your neighbor's house. You shall not covet your neighbor's wife, or his manservant or maidservant, his ox or donkey, or anything that belongs to your neighbor" (Exod. 20:17).

God had just given Himself completely to Israel in holy matrimony. He had said, "I do," promising to take care of

His wife in every way. Why should she covet anything else when she had Him? He longed to be everything to her! Why wouldn't He then expect Israel to trust Him and not feel the need to steal or take from others?

Finally, the Lord said to Israel, "You shall not give false testimony against your neighbor" (Exod. 20:16). What has to be understood about this commandment, as well as all the others, is that God was not calling His people just to obey His words but to *do* what He *is*. Because "God is not a man, that he should lie, nor a son of man, that he should change his mind" (Num. 23:19), He wanted His wife to represent Him accurately and to be truthful in her dealings with others.

While this way of thinking about the Ten Commandments coincides with the *proposal* God gave Israel on Mount Sinai, some of you may be having a hard time dealing with all of this bridal language and imagery. Your minds may even be spinning from having to deal with this unique way of looking at the Scriptures and picturing them as an unfolding revelation of the divine romance between God and human beings.

I fully understand. What complicates matters is the fact that many of us have stumbled over some of the questionable content of the Old Testament.* We've especially struggled with the various accounts involving acts of violence and bloodshed. This is why it is so difficult for us to believe that much of the Old Testament is really about a marriage between God and Israel.

Furthermore, the language of the Old Testament period seems rather strange to us. Filled with Hebrew poetry and all kinds of metaphors, its ancient Near Eastern way of thinking is difficult for us to grasp. The Old Testament also contains numerous lists of tribes and foreign nations, many different genealogies, and a chronology that embraces thousands of years of history. All of these issues combined have left a lot of us believing the Old Testament is rather boring and unattractive.

It has also been very difficult for us as Christians living in the West to truly understand the Hebrew mind. This dilemma is largely due to the fact that because we have grown up in Western society, we have been predominantly exposed to and influenced by the philosophical thinking of the ancient Greeks, especially Plato. Over the centuries, a huge cultural divide has been created, separating the West from the East.

GREEK PHILOSOPHY VS. THE HEBREW MIND

During the beginning of the Christian period, a Western worldview began to reshape the thinking of the church. Although the church had been born in a thoroughly Hebrew culture, the influence of Greek philosophy began to erode the very foundation on which Christianity had been established. By the middle of the second century, the church was already leaving its Jewish roots and embracing a Greek worldview.*

For example, Justin Martyr, one of the early church fathers, had been greatly influenced by the famous Greek philosopher Plato. After Martyr became a Christian, he introduced many of Plato's ideas into his own teaching. As the Hebrew Scriptures were used to bring Jews to Christ, Martyr used the thoughts of Plato to reach the Greeks. The following century, Clement and others from Alexandria would place an even greater emphasis on the reading of the Bible through the eyes of Plato.

Origen, the father of Christian theology, was also a Greek philosopher who taught at the school of Alexandria. The widespread influence of Plato on the history of Christian thought can't be overstated. Through the centuries, Greek philosophy and the writings of Plato would have dire consequences for the church, especially in the way many would come to view life, salvation, spirituality, and marriage.

Plato believed that there were two worlds: the visible, material world and the invisible, spiritual world. The worlds were opposite and opposed to each other. Because the visible world was imperfect and a source of evil, the material world was inferior to the spiritual world.[1]

Plato taught that the human soul originated in the heavenly realm, from which it fell into the realm of matter. Though human beings found themselves related to both worlds, they longed for release from their physical bodies so their souls might take flight back to the heavenly world.

Plato also likened the human body to a prison for the soul. The immortal soul (pure spirit) was incarcerated in a defective body of disintegrating clay. He believed salvation would come at death, when the soul escaped the body and soared heavenward to the invisible realm of bliss.

Unlike the ancient Greeks, the Jews viewed the world as good. Though fallen, it was created by a loving God who designed it with man's best interests at heart. Instead of fleeing the world, man is called to experience God's fellowship, love, and passion in the world. According to

Hebrew thought, the created world is not evil nor is it opposed to the spiritual world.

To the Hebrew mind, a human being is a living soul, called to love God passionately within the physical world. Man is not a spirit who has a soul and lives in a body. The "spirit" of man refers to the image of God in man, as well as to the life principle. To the Jew, a man's soul is referring to one's life and is never to be thought of as just a part of man. When God formed man out of the dust of the ground and breathed His life into him, man became a living soul— a living, breathing being.

Greek philosophy also brought in its wake an emphasis on asceticism. This approach to life is still present in varying degrees in the church today. Asceticism advocates a debasement of life. Because the body with its physical appetites is considered evil, it must constantly be policed by rules and regulations. Therefore, a person must seek to avoid anything enjoyable that may prove a hindrance to one's spiritual life. Abstaining from various physical and material pleasures through dietary restrictions, forfeiting possessions, self-imposed silence and seclusion are thought to bring mastery over one's body.

Although rejected by Paul, the ascetic attitude of "Do not touch, do not taste, do not handle" (Col. 2:21, NKJV) remains deeply embedded in the history of Christian thinking. At the time of the Reformation, Christianity was being defined as abstaining from cheese and butter for Lent rather than by loving one's neighbor.

John Wesley, the evangelist and father of the Methodist movement, even taught a form of asceticism in his *theology of perfection*. He wrote, "Beware of desiring anything but God ... Admit no desire of pleasing food, or any other

60

pleasures of sense; no desire of pleasing the eye or imagination by anything grand, or new or beautiful ... [no desire] of happiness in any creature."[2]

On the surface, the ascetic approach to life appears deeply spiritual. However, the overall theme of Scripture reflects a totally different way of thinking. Many good things can be abused and even come between a person and God (1 Tim. 6:9-10). Anyone can become mastered by physical passions and material possessions. But the biblical solution is not an ascetic denial of such things; instead, we are encouraged to enjoy and celebrate the Lord's incredible gifts with gratitude and humility.

For the Jews, spirituality did not mean just turning inward; true devotion was not simply the private nurturing of certain godly disciplines. Instead, true spirituality meant being fully human, with every fiber of a person being alive and empowered in passionate service to God and humanity. The Hebrew people were never encouraged to be indifferent or bland about life.

There was no distinction between the spiritual and the secular areas of life. It was all God's world, and it was to be enjoyed without a sense of guilt and shame. As stewards of God's creation, human beings were to live in the world and use it according to God's purposes.

Manual labor was elevated to a place of dignity and respect. The Jews saw their God-given vocations as a means of bringing honor to the Lord by the very act of work itself. To work was to worship. The ancient Hebrews made no distinction between sacred and non-sacred occupations. This is why Paul wrote, "Whatever you do, work at it with all your heart, as working for the Lord, not for men" (Col. 3:23).

When Christians become too focused on simply enjoying the pleasures of the world to come, they minimize the importance of the present, short-lived opportunity to glorify God in their lives right now. Satisfaction and pleasure are not to be viewed as ends in themselves. Yet the enjoyment of the physical and material aspects of life is an opportunity to bring pleasure to the heart of God. "So whether you eat or drink or whatever you do, do it all for the glory of God" (1 Cor. 10:31).

Greek philosophy also taught that the human body is inferior to the soul. The Greeks believed the body and soul were constantly at war with each other. The body was corruptible and the source of sin. Once the original Jewish leadership of the church was replaced by Gentiles, even marriage began to be viewed in a negative light and as an inferior way of life.

Monks, living under a vow of chastity, were considered close to God because they denied themselves certain physical pleasures. Priests, having embraced a life of celibacy, were put on a pedestal for denying the "sinful desires of the body." Some Gnostics went so far as to teach that marriage was a "foul and polluted way of life" and that eternal life could not be obtained if one remained in this kind of relationship.

Augustine (fifth century) suggested that the Jewish patriarchs would have preferred to fulfill God's command to "be fruitful and multiply" without indulging in intercourse. But since this was obviously impossible, Augustine believed that they must have had sexual relations with their wives only reluctantly and out of duty. Martin Luther viewed marriage primarily as a cure for the uncontrollable sexual desire troubling every human being.

The Bible, however, clearly affirms that marriage is holy, honorable, and undefiled (1 Tim. 4:3-4; Heb. 13:4). The Jews did not consider the body and its appetites as evil or shameful. They didn't teach that celibacy was the ideal state or the highest kind of human existence. Instead, Song of Solomon celebrates human love and sexuality in bold terms.

Also, during the Middle Ages, the concept of salvation revolved around "being taken out of this world." Salvation came when one was delivered from this life. During medieval times there were many victims of poverty, hunger, disease, and violence. Since some longed to escape from a corrupt world, this other-worldly theology appeared attractive and actually still remains a compelling option today.

In contrast, the Jews did not primarily view salvation as deliverance from this world. Their desire was not to escape this life but to know God and experience His power and presence, which would transform both their lives and their society. The Hebrew people understood that to seek deliverance from this life was no permanent solution to the problems of this world. Their identity as God's people compelled them to try to change society and not live in isolation from others. The Jews knew that the highest calling of human beings was to love God and bring Him honor through the work of their hands.

Lastly, many Christians today understand faith primarily as an activity of the mind. For them, to believe or have faith is mainly a matter of intellectual assent to truth. The Jews, however, looked at faith differently. To the Hebrew mind, faith meant faithfulness, a life based on trust. One of the most pivotal passages in the Old Testament is

Habakkuk 2:4: "But the righteous will live by his faith [trusting faithfulness]" (emphasis added).

Faith to the Hebrew people was a life lived out of intimacy with God. It was about a relationship between a Husband and His wife based on trust and fidelity. Faith was about a bride clinging to her Bridegroom in confidence instead of clinging to the fear and uncertainty of the future. The life of faith for the Jews was all about loving God intimately and celebrating life boldly.

John Spong once wrote, "The Bible is a Hebrew book telling the story of the Hebrew people. Jesus was a Hebrew Lord. We, on the other hand, are Western people sharing a very diverse and sometimes controversial heritage that comes from many sources. If the Bible is going to be understood in our day, we must develop 'Hebrew eyes' and 'Hebrew attitudes' toward life."[3]

Today, Western thinking needs to be replaced by Hebrew thinking if we are going to understand the Scriptures the way they were written. The Bible will only make sense to us when we see it as an unfolding love story between a passionate God and human beings who were made in His image.

ENDNOTES

*In embarking on a quest to bring some clarity to the apparent theological tension between the revelation of God unveiled in the Old Covenant and the truth of God's nature revealed in Christ, we first need to be reminded that the Old Testament was an *incomplete* revelation of God's nature. While inspired, it was still a progressive unfolding of God's heart and purpose that would see its fulfillment in the coming of Messiah. One of the primary reasons why Jesus came to earth was to give us a true picture and understanding of the character of God.

Furthermore, to understand some of the language of the Old Testament, we need to be aware of the belief systems of both ancient Israel and the cultures that influenced them. For example, it was *common* in ancient Near Eastern worship to find sacrifices, a priesthood, "holy" places, circumcision, purification rites, and festivals. In his providence, God appropriated certain symbols and rituals familiar to Israel and infused them with new meaning and significance in light of his saving, historical acts and his covenant relationship with Israel (emphasis added).[4]

God worked with the Hebrew people as He found them. He used language and illustrations they could understand. He met them where they were while seeking to show them a higher ideal in the context of ancient Near Eastern life. We can't make sense of their views until we set them against their background and environment.

Throughout the Old Testament, God was laying the groundwork for an ongoing, progressive revelation of Himself that would culminate in the coming of Christ. The focal point of this foundation was monotheism [the belief in only one God]. Because of the polytheistic views of Israel's neighbors, God was consistently emphasizing that He alone is Creator and that He alone is the sovereign Ruler of the whole world. Given this emphasis, the Hebrew writers of Scripture often described events or circumstances as coming from the hand of their Creator. But as we look at the Old Testament through the lens of Christ, it soon becomes apparent that God did not mean that every event was caused by Him or ordained by Him before the beginning of time.

*For a further study of this subject, read *Our Father Abraham*, by Marvin R. Wilson.

CLOSING PRAYER

Father, in the Name of Jesus, I really want my heart awakened to the romance of redemption. Deliver me from any preconceived ideas that would prevent me from truly understanding your heart. And help me understand the Scriptures the way they were written. Amen.

Chapter Six

FOREVER FAITHFUL

The Mount Sinai experience between God and Israel was not only spectacular and beautiful but also sacred and binding. When the Lord proposed to His future wife, He pledged that His covenant loyalty would be as constant as the shining of the sun, moon, and stars (Jer. 31:35-36). He engraved Israel on the palms of His hands (Isa. 49:16) and said to her, "I will betroth you to me forever" (Hosea 2:19).

The marriage between God and His chosen required an exclusive commitment. This commitment ruled out all potential rivals who might compete for their love and affection. At Mount Sinai, the Lord said to Israel, "Out of all nations you will be my treasured possession" (Exod. 19:5). But He also said to her, "You shall have no other gods [lovers] before me" (Exod. 20:3, emphasis added). While some believe that monogamy breeds monotony, a marriage can only thrive when its unity is preserved. Seeking love in the arms of another destroys the oneness of a covenant relationship.

When God *popped the question* to Israel and presented the marriage contract to her, she agreed to the terms of the covenant and vowed to keep her word (Exod. 19:8). To the Jews, one's word was considered equal to one's promise. When Israel said, "I do," she wasn't just vowing to comply externally with various rules or laws. She was promising to love, honor, and obey the One who had entered into marriage with her.

At Mount Sinai, the Lord was not only saying to Israel, "Be My wife," but He was also pledging Himself to her and promising to carry out His covenant obligations as her Husband. According to tradition, the marriage contract (*ketubah*) was a covenant that specified the bride price and other provisions the bridegroom was prepared to make for his bride. On the mountain, God vowed to provide for Israel's every need, as well as honor His wife above all the nations of the earth.

WHAT'S IN A NAME

To reinforce His covenant commitment to His wife, God made Himself known to Israel through various names. In biblical times, one's name was a declaration of one's *character*. Through the different names the Lord chose for Himself, He was conveying to His wife what He meant when He said "I will be your God" in covenant relationship.

YAHWEH YIREH

A number of years after Abraham was invited to embrace a covenant relationship with God, he took a journey with his son to Mount Moriah. The purpose of the trip was to offer Isaac in sacrifice before the Lord. However, just before Isaac was killed, God stopped Abraham: "Abraham looked up and there in a thicket he saw a ram caught by its horns. He went over and took the ram and sacrificed it as a burnt offering instead of his son. So Abraham called that place The Lord Will Provide" (Gen. 22:13-14).

Abraham realized that God had provided another sacrifice, so he named the place *Yahweh Yireh*, which means "The Lord Who Sees," or "The Lord Who Provides." God used this experience on Mount Moriah to reveal to Abraham and his descendants that He truly is a covenant Provider.

In Abraham's day, it was customary for anyone making a covenant to swear by something or someone greater than himself in order to validate the covenant. Often individuals would swear by their king, which meant that the king would intervene if any disputes arose over the terms of the covenant.

But to whom was God going to swear, since there is none greater or more powerful? He could swear by no one other than Himself. This is what is meant in Hebrews 6:

> When God made his promise to Abraham, since there was no one greater for him to swear by, he swore by himself, saying, "I will surely bless you and give you many descendants" ... Men swear by someone greater than themselves, and the oath confirms what is said and puts an end to all argument. Because God wanted to make the unchanging nature of his purpose very clear to the heirs of what was promised, he confirmed it with an oath. God did this so that, by two unchangeable things in which it is impossible for God to lie, we who have fled to take hold of the hope offered to us may be greatly encouraged (Heb. 6:13-14, 16-18).

Think of it. When Abraham needed a sacrifice, God provided one. And in so doing, God was making a promise to Abraham and *all his descendants* to not only provide for their every need, but to offer His own "Isaac" one day for the sins of mankind.

God even foretold of the occasion in the book of Isaiah. Speaking of His Son, the Father promised, "I will appoint You as a *covenant* to the people, as a light to the nations, to open blind eyes, to bring out prisoners from the dungeon" (Isa. 42:6-7, NASB, italics added).

God has made a covenant on our behalf and has sent Jesus to be the guarantee and the messenger of the covenant (Heb. 7:22; Mal. 3:1). Because of this, the fulfillment of everything contained in the covenant is absolutely guaranteed. God cannot lie! As the Faithful One, God always carries out His covenant responsibilities perfectly. He is forever "The Lord Who Sees and Provides."

YAHWEH ROPH'EKA

After the Hebrew people had been delivered from Egypt and had crossed the Red Sea, they found themselves in the desert without water for three days. When they eventually discovered water, they realized it was bitter and undrinkable. As Moses cried to the Lord on behalf of the people, God showed him a tree. When Moses cast the tree into the bitter water, the water became sweet.

It was there at Marah that God gave His people a profound promise: "If you listen carefully to the voice of the Lord your God and do what is right in his eyes, if you pay attention to his commands and keep all his decrees, I will not bring on you any of the diseases I brought on the Egyptians, for I am the Lord, who heals you" (Exod. 15:26).

It was at this same time that God revealed Himself to Israel as her Physician. Through the redemptive name, *Yahweh Roph'eka*, which means "The Lord Your Healer," God pledged to meet all of Israel's physical needs as she loved and obeyed Him.

We also need to notice how soon this experience took place after the departure of the Hebrew people from Egypt. God made Himself known to Israel as her Healer at the beginning of her journey to the land of Canaan. The first promise God made to her after the crossing of the Red Sea was the promise of healing.

The pledge made to Israel in Exodus 15:26 is relevant to us because God was forever expressing His heart's desire, as well as His character to His people. All that He would make known of Himself through His various names under the Older Covenant would later be fulfilled in Christ. James 1:17 tells us that God "does not change like shifting shadows." This simply means that God doesn't change even slightly. If the Lord was *Yahweh Roph'eka* under the Older Covenant, it's impossible to view Christ as Someone other than our Healer under the New Covenant.

Also, the tree God showed to Moses was actually symbolic of Jesus' death on the cross. Through the finished work of Christ, the "bitter" effects of sin (including sickness) were removed (Isa. 53:4; Matt. 8:16-17). Just as it was necessary for Moses to cast the tree into the bitter water, it's essential for us to appropriate by faith the promises the Lord has provided through the cross.

Furthermore, Israel's journey out of Egypt and through the Red Sea was symbolic of our redemption and deliverance from sin and all its power. Just as God encouraged His people at the beginning of their journey with the promise of healing and health, it's still God's desire to encourage us at the start of our Christian experience with the same promise.[1]

YAHWEH NISSI

In their journey from Egypt to Canaan, the people of God came to a place called Rephidim, where they encountered the Amalekites, Esau's descendants. The Israelites were already discouraged because after arriving at Rephidim, they discovered there was no water to drink. They became so distraught that they said, "Is the Lord among us or not?" (Exod. 17:7). The people really needed courage to face their enemies and the dangers that lay ahead.

In the ensuing battle, the Lord was with Israel, and they eventually defeated the Amalekites. Afterward, "Moses built an altar and called it The Lord is my Banner" (Exod. 17:15). It was there at Rephidim that God revealed Himself to His people as *Yahweh Nissi*, "The Lord Your Banner— Guarantee of Victory."

Like Israel, Joshua also knew what it was to be distraught and afraid. For years he had been Moses' right-hand man. But after Moses' death, Joshua realized that it was his turn to lead. He understood that Israel wasn't just going to waltz into the Promised Land; they were going to have to fight for it. And Moses wasn't going with them.

If Joshua had been completely confident about the situation, why did the Lord have to tell him over and over again to be strong and courageous? In fact, God had to give him a special word of encouragement: "As I was with Moses, so I will be with you; I will never leave you nor forsake you" (Josh. 1:5).

How was God with Moses? The Lord was with Moses and encouraged him as *Yahweh Nissi*, "The Lord Your Banner." Then God covenanted with Joshua to do the same, and Israel took down Jericho and overcame their enemies.

The covenant pledge that God gave Israel really opens up the riches of the promises Christ gave when He boldly declared, "I am with you always, even to the end of the age" and "I will never leave you nor forsake you" (Matt. 28:20; Heb. 13:5, NKJV). These promises aren't suggesting that Jesus is just going to show up and comfort us in our troubles. We are in union with Him, and we're seated with Him in heavenly places far above all principalities and powers (Eph. 1:15-23). His pledge to us means that we don't have anything to fear. He will always be, "The Lord Our Banner—Guarantee of Victory!"

YAHWEH SHALOM

When Gideon feared for his life because he had seen the Angel of the Lord face to face, the Lord of the covenant spoke to him and said: "'Peace! Do not be afraid. You are not going to die.' So Gideon built an altar to the Lord there and called it The Lord is Peace" (Judg. 6:23-24). It was at Ophrah that God made Himself known to Gideon as *Yahweh Shalom*.

God longed to be everything to His people and expressed His heart's desire even further in Psalm 29:10-11. "The Lord sits enthroned over the flood; the Lord is enthroned as King forever. The Lord gives strength to his people; the Lord blesses his people with peace." God wanted Israel to walk in His covenant of peace. This is why He exalted Himself as King over the covenant, guaranteeing that every promise would be fulfilled on His people's behalf. It was in this passage that the Lord used vivid Hebrew, poetic language to describe His rule over every flood that would threaten to drown His wife.

In the same way, Jesus is "The Lord Our Peace." His invitation to us is "Do not be anxious about anything, but in everything, by prayer and petition, with thanksgiving, present your requests to God. And the peace of God, which transcends all understanding, will guard your hearts and your minds in Christ Jesus" (Phil. 4:6-7).

Jesus is exalted as King over the flood of our pain and sorrow, loneliness and despair, sickness and disease, weakness and inability. As the great I AM, He *is* our strength and peace in times of trial and temptation. We can rest assured that He is more committed to us than we will ever be to Him.

To each of us, the King says,

> Fear not, for I have redeemed you; I have summoned you by name; you are mine. When you pass through the waters, I will be with you; and when you pass through the rivers, they will not sweep over you. When you walk through the fire, you will not be burned; the flames will not set you ablaze. For I am the Lord, your God, the Holy One

of Israel, your Savior … Since you are precious and honored in my sight, and because I love you, I will give men in exchange for you, and people in exchange for your life. Do not be afraid, for I am with you (Isa. 43:1-5).

YAHWEH SHAMMAH

When Israel found herself in Babylonian captivity because of her sin, the Lord revealed Himself to her as *Yahweh Shammah*, "The Lord Who Is There." The promise contained in this name was given to a wife who was at her lowest point spiritually. "By the rivers of Babylon we sat and wept when we remembered Zion. There on the poplars we hung our harps, for there our captors asked us for songs, our tormentors demanded songs of joy; they said, 'Sing us one of the songs of Zion!' How can we sing the songs of the Lord while in a foreign land?" (Ps. 137:1-4).

It was to His broken wife that the Lord pledged to build a city, a place of His dwelling where He would be in her midst. And He said to her, "The name of the city from that time on will be: The Lord Is There" (Ezek. 48:35).

For those of us who may be broken by sin and the consequences of poor choices, the Lord pledges to be there for us. He is forever faithful to renew our hearts and give us hope. Mercy and grace are always available to us, even at our lowest point spiritually. As Brian Longridge has so beautifully written: "Your deepest, darkest place can become an embryo of Eternal Beauty, for Grace knows how to dance in the depths."

YAHWEH TSIDKENU

In Jeremiah 23, the God of the covenant made Himself known to Israel as *Yahweh Tsidkenu*, "The Lord Our Righteousness." But notice the context in which He revealed Himself to her by that name. Hear His heart's cry: "'Woe to the shepherds who are destroying and scattering the sheep of my pasture!' declares the Lord" (Jer. 23:1).

The prophet Jeremiah felt the pure passion and love of God for His wife and was deeply grieved over the abominable sins of the prophets and priests. He couldn't hold back the emotion:

> Concerning the prophets: My heart is broken within me; all my bones tremble. I am like a drunken man, like a man overcome by wine, because of the Lord and his holy words. The land is full of adulterers; because of the curse the land lies parched and the pastures in the desert are withered. The prophets follow an evil course and use their power unjustly. "Both prophet and priest are godless; even in my temple I find their wickedness," declares the Lord (Jer. 23: 9-11).

As God's mouthpiece, the prophet Ezekiel reinforced Jeremiah's complaint:

> Woe to the shepherds of Israel who only take care of themselves! Should not shepherds take care of the flock? You eat the curds, clothe yourselves with the wool and slaughter the choice animals, but you do not take care of the flock. You have not

strengthened the weak or healed the sick or bound up the injured. You have not brought back the strays or searched for the lost. You have ruled them harshly and brutally (Ezek. 34:2-4).

The shepherds of Israel were using and abusing God's wife instead of serving her. They were more interested in their own gain than in nurturing and caring for her. Out of holy passion, the Lord warned them: "Because you have scattered my flock and driven them away and have not bestowed care on them, I will bestow punishment on you for the evil you have done" (Jer.23:2).

The Lord then comforted Israel with these words:

"I myself will gather the remnant of my flock out of all the countries where I have driven them and will bring them back to their pasture, where they will be fruitful and increase in number. I will place shepherds over them who will tend them, and they will no longer be afraid or terrified, nor will any be missing," declares the Lord. "The days are coming," declares the Lord, "when I will raise up to David a righteous Branch, a King who will reign wisely and do what is just and right in the land. In his days Judah will be saved and Israel will live in safety. This is the name by which he will be called: The Lord Our Righteousness" (Jer. 23:3-6).

To the Jewish mind, *righteousness* is a term that always speaks of relationship. When we talk about the righteousness of God, we are speaking about the utter "rightness" of the relationship between the Father, Son, and Holy Spirit. Yet what is essential for us to understand is that through the finished work of the cross, we are now in right relationship with the Father, Jesus, and the Holy Spirit.

The free gift of *righteousness* given to us through Christ displays the life that God always had in mind for us. We have been brought face-to-face before Him, fully identified with Jesus in blameless innocence. The flawless redemption of Christ has ushered us into a flawless fellowship!

The early church fathers used a Greek word to describe the intimate relationship that takes place within the Godhead. The Greek word is *perichoresis*. It is derived from the word *peri*, which means "around" and the word *chorea*, which means "dance." Think of it—the Father, Son, and Holy Spirit in complete unity in a "divine dance." But the mystery of it all is that through the finished work of Christ, each of us has been invited to the dance. This dance celebrates our perfect union and fellowship with God. The *rhythm* that man lost in the Garden has been restored to us.

This is why it is so important for Christian leaders to properly represent the heart of the Bridegroom to the bride and to make her aware of all that He has accomplished on her behalf. Today, there are far too many preachers who *use* the bride of Christ for their own gain. Instead of finding their identity as friends of the Bridegroom, they find their identity in their ministries. They continually use the people of God to fulfill their personal destinies.

There are also ministries that abuse the bride through heavy-handed leadership styles, manipulation, and control. *Fear* is used as the primary motivation for keeping the people in line. In a number of churches, isolated Old

Testament passages relating to the judgment of a wicked, adulterous Israel are used to scare immature Christians into staying on the straight and narrow.

In 1 Corinthians 3, Paul admonishes those in church leadership about the importance of serving faithfully for the *building up* of God's people. He admonishes the "shepherds" that if they build on the foundation of Jesus Christ with inferior materials, their works will be consumed by the fire of God's love for His bride (1 Cor. 3:12-13, 15). Although these verses have been used to admonish Christians in general about their works for the Lord, this passage is primarily addressing leaders and their methods and motivations for ministry.

This same admonition is echoed by James in his letter to the church. "Not many of you should presume to be teachers, my brothers, because you know that we who teach will be judged more strictly" (James 3:1). It's imperative for pastors and leaders to understand that they have been entrusted with the awesome privilege and responsibility of loving and serving the bride of Christ.

Even now, the Holy Spirit is raising up "friends of the Bridegroom" who have a heart to serve and care for the bride of Christ. These individuals are finding their true joy in loving Jesus and celebrating the intimacy between the Bridegroom and His bride (John 3:29). Instead of experiencing their ultimate satisfaction in the ministry, these men and women are modeling true leadership in the spirit of humility and servanthood. They bear the heart of the Righteous Lord and burn with His love for the bride.

YAHWEH M'KADDESH

The Lord gave Israel another incredible covenant promise when He revealed Himself to her as *Yahweh M'kaddesh*, "The Lord Who Sanctifies." This promise is found in Leviticus 20:7-8: "Consecrate yourselves and be holy, because I am the Lord your God. Keep my decrees and follow them. I am the Lord, who makes you holy."

The heart of these verses is vividly portrayed for us in Ezekiel 16. Remember, the ancient Jewish wedding consisted of two parts, beginning with a betrothal or engagement. Once the bride-to-be agreed to the terms of the marriage contract, she was sanctified or set apart for her husband.

Through the passion and poetry of the Hebrew language, God beautifully illustrated the intimate details of what took place between Him and His wife, Israel.

> "Later I passed by, and when I looked at you and saw that you were old enough for love, I spread the corner of my garment over you and covered your nakedness. I gave you my solemn oath and entered into a covenant with you," declares the Sovereign Lord, "and you became mine. I bathed you with water and washed the blood from you and put ointments on you" (Ezek. 16:8-9).

When Israel said "I do" and pledged herself to the Lord, she was set apart just for Him. He sanctified her. He washed off her blood and anointed her with fragrant oils. But in order for us to grasp the full impact of what is being said here, we have to understand that it was *menstrual blood* that the Lord washed off His wife.

Isaiah 64:6 reminds us that "All of us have become like one who is unclean, and all our righteous acts are like filthy rags." However, the Hebrew phrase for "filthy rags" is far more explicit. It literally means "garments of menstruation." Think about it. God chooses a wife, and then one day He kneels before her in utter humility. He washes off her menstrual blood and covers her shame with His love. He replaces her filthy menstrual cloths with His righteousness and clothes her with His splendor and beauty (Ezek. 16:10-14). And she becomes His queen!

The Lord, in His grace and mercy, also chose us for Himself. He entered into a covenant with us. We are His bride. He sanctified us and set us apart to enjoy Him forever. He stooped down and washed off our sin. He replaced our filthy rags with His righteousness. He clothed us with His beautiful perfections, and we stand before Him just as if we had never sinned (1 Cor. 1:30). As "The Lord Who Sanctifies," Jesus will remain forever faithful and committed to us until we see Him face to face.

CLOSING PRAYER

Father, in the Name of Jesus, I'm overwhelmed by Your great love for me. And Jesus, what can I say? Your sacrifice for me is beyond comprehension. Help me to live out of the comfort and security of knowing that You will always be there for me. I want my obedience to be a response of love to You. Thank You for being forever faithful to me. Amen.

Chapter Seven

GOD—
THE PASSIONATE HUSBAND

After God created the pure, passionate union between Adam and Eve, He turned the world upside down when He indicated that this is the kind of relationship He has always wanted with man. In fact, the Apostle Paul clearly states that this is one of the primary reasons why the Lord created men and women, marriage and sexuality—to serve as a living illustration for all of us. He quoted from the book of Genesis and then took it to another level: "'For this reason a man will leave his father and mother and be united to his wife, and the two will become one flesh.' This is a profound mystery—but I am talking about Christ and the church" (Eph. 5:31-32).

It is a profound mystery indeed. But we have to see the Bible for what it is—the record of the greatest romance ever! God created man for intimacy with Himself. As we've already seen, He even romanced a nation and entered into a marriage covenant with her. He told her she was the apple of His eye and pledged to be everything to her.

But that wasn't good enough for Israel. Some time after the honeymoon, God's wife started having wandering eyes. She found herself attracted to the gods of the surrounding nations and became titillated by the lure of pagan worship. The gods of the other religions weren't restrictive like her Husband. The pagan deities encouraged temple prostitution as a part of the religious rituals. Sexual orgies were commonplace, and men could even engage in sex with men as well as women.

It's true that the Lord had always been good to His wife. Without Him she would never have attained what she had. No one had wanted Israel except God. He had protected her and taken care of all her needs, though she frequently murmured and complained. He hadn't turned His back on her even when she desired to be back in Egypt. He stood by her side and never budged, proving His faithfulness to her time and time again.

But from Israel's perspective, His predictability may have been a big part of the problem. While faithfulness is essential for the health of a relationship, it doesn't appear flashy or fascinating. To some, faithfulness can even seem drab and dull. After all, faithfulness is, by definition, predictable and routine. Philip Yancey writes:

> I remember my first visit to Old Faithful in Yellowstone National Park. Rings of Japanese and German tourists surrounded the geyser, their video cameras trained like weapons on the famous hole in the ground. A large digital clock stood beside the spot, predicting twenty-four minutes before the next eruption.
>
> My wife and I passed the countdown in the dining room of Old Faithful Inn overlooking the geyser. When the digital clock reached one minute, we, along with every other diner, left our seats and rushed to the windows to see the big, wet event.

I noticed immediately, as if on signal, a crew of busboys and waiters descended on the tables to refill water glasses and clear away dirty dishes. When the geyser went off, we tourists oohed and aahed and clicked our cameras; a few spontaneously applauded. But, glancing back over my shoulder, I saw that not a single waiter or busboy—not even those who had finished their chores—looked out the huge windows. Old Faithful, grown entirely too familiar, had lost its power to impress them.[1]

I believe Israel got bored with God. She got tired of His ways. She didn't want to be tied down to her Husband. For her, monogamy had bred monotony. She believed she was missing out on the passion and pleasure of having other lovers, so she went after the gods of the other nations shamelessly. Even though the Lord had wooed and pursued her, it wasn't enough. And she broke His heart!

You can actually feel the pain in the Lord's response to Israel:

"I remember the devotion of your youth, how as a bride you loved me and followed me through the desert, through a land not sown. Israel was holy to the Lord ... But my people have exchanged their Glory for worthless idols. Be appalled at this, O heavens, and shudder with great horror," declares the Lord. "My people have committed two sins: They have forsaken me, the spring of living water, and have dug their own cisterns, broken cisterns that cannot hold water" (Jer. 2:2-3, 11-13).

And again: "'And your fame spread among the nations on account of your beauty, because the splendor I had given you made your beauty perfect,' declares the Sovereign Lord. 'But you trusted in your beauty and used your fame to become a prostitute. You lavished your favors on anyone who passed by and your beauty became his'" (Ezek. 16:14-15).

The Lord's pain turned into pure passion. He even went so far as to compare His wife to a female donkey in heat: "See how you behaved in the valley; consider what you have done. You are a swift she-camel running here and there, a wild donkey accustomed to the desert, sniffing the wind in her craving—in her heat who can restrain her? Any males that pursue her need not tire themselves; at mating time they will find her" (Jer. 2:23-24).

God admonished His wandering wife like a lover who had been rejected: "Because you have forgotten me and trusted in false gods, I will pull up your skirts over your face that your shame may be seen—your adulteries and lustful neighing, your shameless prostitution!" (Jer. 13:25-27).

JUSTIFIABLY JEALOUS

Over the years, numerous people have stumbled over God's anger and wrath. The issue of judgment has been both misunderstood and maligned. What so many have failed to comprehend is the fact that the Lord has always burned with *pure* passion for the undivided love and devotion of His people. And why should this come as a surprise to us? As the Hero and Husband in the love story called the Bible, the Lord has always wanted His wife to be lovingly devoted to Him. Is this too much for Him to ask? What kind of husband would He be if He expected anything less?

Men, how would you feel if you fell head over heels in love with a woman and you married her, only to discover later that while you were at work trying to provide for her every need, she was opening up your bedroom for *anyone* who would have her? What kind of emotions would your wife's betrayal arouse in you? How would you feel if she took the dresses and perfumes you had given her and used them to make herself more attractive to other men?

Yet, this is exactly what Israel did. She flaunted her fornication in the face of her Husband and used the gifts He had lavished on her to make herself more appealing and attractive to the gods of the other nations. Israel's deeds were deplorable and shameless. And to make matters worse, she wasn't even picky concerning those with whom she went to bed.

The Lord was brokenhearted and let His wife know it:

> "You took some of your garments to make gaudy high places, where you carried on your prostitution. Such things should not happen, nor should they ever occur. You also took the fine jewelry I gave you, the jewelry made of my gold and silver, and you made for yourself male idols and engaged in prostitution with them. And you took your embroidered clothes to put on them, and you offered my oil and incense before them … In all your detestable

practices and prostitution you did not remember the days of your youth, when you
were naked and bare, kicking about in your
blood. Woe! Woe to you," declares the
Sovereign Lord (Ezek. 16: 16-18, 22-23).

To truly grasp the significance of the Lord's *spirited*
response to His wife's unfaithfulness, we have to understand something about His holy jealousy. It's very eye-
opening to discover how much the Scriptures have to say
about the subject:

- "Do not worship any other god, for the Lord, whose
  name is Jealous, is a jealous God" (Exod. 34:14).

- "For the Lord your God is a consuming fire, a
  jealous God" (Deut. 4: 24).

- "They made me jealous by what is no god and
  angered me with their worthless idols" (Deut. 32:
  21).

- "They angered him with their high places; they
  aroused his jealousy with their idols" (Ps. 78:58).

There are also numerous other passages that speak of
the Lord's jealousy for His people. (See Num. 25:11; Josh.
24:19; Ps. 79:5; Ezek. 8:3; 16:38, 42; 23:25; 36:5; 39:25;
Joel 2:18; Nah. 1:2; Zeph. 1:18; 3:8; Zech. 1:14; 8:2; Jas.
4:4-5).

But exactly what does the Bible mean when it speaks of
God's jealousy? How can he be the epitome of love and be
jealous at the same time? Some people may be repulsed by
the thought that God might be affected by such a terrible

flaw of character, because all of us, at one time or another, have been on the receiving end of human jealousy that was both devastating and destructive.

To say that the Lord is jealous most certainly does not mean He is suspicious because of some insecurity on His part. How can this be said of the One who is infinitely perfect in every way?

Ungodly jealousy is the by-product of wanting to control and possess what does not belong to us. It is always demanding and cares very little about the alleged object of its love.

In contrast, holy jealousy is at the very core of who God is. Within the depths of His being burns an inextinguishable fire of love called jealousy. His jealousy is a blazing passion to protect a *love relationship* that is eternally precious to Him and to defend it when it is broken. Divine jealousy is that unbridled energy in God which stirs Him to take action against whatever stands in the way of His relationship with those He loves and desires.

While the Lord is purely jealous for His bride, He is not jealous on His behalf. He wants the very best for her. When He sees His bride giving her heart to things that could cause her harm, He immediately becomes jealous for her safety.

In his book *The Misunderstood God*, Darin Hufford writes, "God is a jealous God, but He is jealous on behalf of you. He is not selfishly jealous as human beings are. His righteous jealousy is actually the opposite of what we understand jealousy to be. Until we understand this principle of God's heart, we will always see Him upside down from what He really is. We have taken the Scriptures that describe Him as a jealous God and have given them a selfish and Satanlike interpretation. It has become so common that we don't even recognize it anymore."[2]

WHAT'S UP WITH GOD'S WRATH?

The measure of God's jealousy is in direct proportion to the depths of His love for those who belong to Him. Furthermore, His anger is never irrational and unpredictable. His wrath is not uncontrollable fury and violence.

Although the word *anger* is usually synonymous with recklessness and rage, the biblical term refers to what we would call *righteous indignation*. God's anger and wrath are aroused by what He considers destructive to His people. However, the Lord's anger is a *secondary* emotion and never the ruling passion of His heart.

Furthermore, according to Jewish tradition, God's anger and wrath must also be viewed as *suspended mercy*. In other words, He "judges" men's sins by reluctantly letting them have what they want. This is vividly illustrated for us in Romans 1:18-28. When Paul wrote that God gave men over to sexual immorality (v.24), shameful lusts (v.26), and a depraved mind (v.28), he wasn't suggesting that God was the source of such things. Instead, Paul was stating that because men wanted to continue to engage in wickedness, the Lord had to suspend His mercy by allowing them to suffer the consequences of their sins. *But He detested what He had to allow!*

God's love for Israel was the source of His anger and wrath. It was because He infinitely cared for His wife that He burned with holy jealousy for her. It angered Him that sin and Satan were able to repeatedly devastate and destroy His people because of the choices they had made.

Anger and mercy are not opposites of each other; they are actually related. This is why the prophet Habakkuk prayed: "in wrath remember mercy" (Hab. 3:2). It is inconceivable that the Lord's love would ever end. This is why the psalmist asked: "Has God forgotten to be merciful? Has he in anger withheld his compassion?" (Ps. 77:9).

There is an evil that many today condone and even tolerate. It's the evil of *indifference*. However, any indifference to evil is more insidious than the evil itself. God, on the other hand, is not indifferent to evil. He is always concerned. He is personally affected by what man does. He is a God of sympathy. The anger of the Lord is really the opposite of indifference.

It is also impossible to understand the meaning of divine anger without considering the significance of divine patience. Clearly, the Bible reveals that God is patient, longsuffering, and slow to anger (Exod. 34:6; Num. 14:18; Ps. 86:15; 103:8; 145:8; Jer. 15:15; Joel 2:13). However the Lord's patience is never to be confused with apathy or indifference. The patience of God is His restraint of *justifiable* anger.

The message of God's anger included a call to His adulterous wife to return to Him and be restored. If she changed her behavior and came back to Him, He would no longer suspend His mercy and allow her to suffer the consequences of her unfaithfulness. The call of anger was really a call to cancel anger. It was not an expression of irrational behavior but a deliberate response on God's part to deal with what was evil and destructive to His wife.

For all its passion, the Lord's anger could be averted by His wife's change of heart. There was never any divine anger for anger's sake. Although God was forced to withdraw His protective presence because of His wife's repeated adultery, it was always in His heart to see her come to a place of repentance. Beyond divine justice and anger was the *mystery* of the Lord's compassion.

MOMENTARY ANGER

In Scripture, God's anger is always described as something temporary rather than something that lasts indefinitely. This is reinforced for us by the prophet Micah: "Who is a God like you, who pardons sin and forgives the transgression of the remnant of his inheritance? You do not stay angry forever but delight to show mercy" (Mic. 7:18).

The psalmist David also spoke of the Lord's anger as being temporary: "For his anger lasts only a moment, but his favor lasts a lifetime; weeping may remain for a night, but rejoicing comes in the morning" (Ps. 30:5).

When Israel asked the question, "Will you always be angry?" (Jer. 3:5), the Lord's response was decisive: "Return, faithless Israel ... I will frown on you no longer, for I am merciful ... I will not be angry forever" (Jer. 3:12).

The secret to understanding God's anger is to understand His *care*. There is nothing greater than the *certainty* of His care. This is confirmed for us through the words of Isaiah: "In that day you will say: 'I will praise You, O Lord. Although you were angry with me, your anger has turned away and you have comforted me'" (Isa. 12:1).

Anger is not an emotion in which God delights. "For he does not willingly bring affliction or grief to the children of men" (Lam. 3:33). The desire of God was to see Israel flourish as a pleasant vine and to be able to say to her, "Fury is not in Me" (Isa. 27:4, NKJV). This is why the Lord asked, "Why do you commit this great evil against yourselves ... in that you provoke me to wrath?" (Jer. 44:7-8, NKJV).

When Israel wanted to be like the other nations and desired an earthly king to rule over her, the Lord told His friend Samuel to warn her about the terrible consequences of forsaking Him (1 Sam. 8:8-18). In fact, 1 and 2 Samuel, 1 and 2 Kings, and 1 and 2 Chronicles describe in detail the stark contrast between what God's wife could have experienced if she would have stayed by His side and loved Him and what she ended up suffering because she left Him for another.

In my book, *ENJOYING GOD*, I write:

> While the Lord is the sovereign ruler of the universe, He has to honor the way He has designed things in the created order by permitting human beings the right to choose what they desire, even though He knows there will be calamitous consequences for the wrong decisions they make. Still it *angers* Him that sin and Satan are able to wreak havoc on individuals, as well as on the world. Because He is so intricately involved in human affairs, He even takes responsibility for what He must allow. Although it appears that He is the source of violence, He merely allows violent beings to do what they choose. But

> God's ultimate purpose in suspending His
> mercy is to bring redemption to those who cry
> out to Him in their anguish and suffering.[3]

Throughout the Scriptures, God's anger was evidence of His deep, passionate concern for His wayward wife. It was a compassion that transcended the purist anger; it was a love that remained steadfast in the face of human sin and weakness. And this is the splendor of God's love and concern that was revealed through the prophets.

PROPHETS—FRIENDS OF THE BRIDEGROOM

The prophets were guided by an intense *intimate* concern for God's concerns. They were more than just mere messengers or spokesmen for God. They were individuals who experienced His love for His wife in the very depths of their beings. The prophets were deeply moved, not by what they felt, but by what the Lord felt. Their words were really an unloading of the Lord's burden. This is why you find the phrase, "the burden of the Lord," frequently used throughout their writings.

For some people, the very thought of God's anger is repulsive. They equate it with pain and suffering. For God, however, the anger *is* pain. His anger expressed in the Bible was rooted in the sorrow and suffering He endured because of Israel's disloyalty. And the prophets uniquely shared in the tension between God's love and His holy displeasure.

I used to think the prophets were guys with long, pointed bony fingers who loved getting in people's faces with their "turn or burn" message. I later realized that it wasn't about that at all. As friends of the Bridegroom, they literally felt the jealousy of the Lord for His adulterous wife. This helped me understand the zeal of the prophets and their emotional oneness with God.

This is what the prophet Samuel must have experienced when Israel told him that she wanted another king to rule over her instead of the Lord. It appears that Samuel felt God's pain so strongly that he took Israel's rejection of God *personally*. This is why "the Lord told him: 'Listen to all that the people are saying to you; it is not you they have rejected, but they have rejected me as their king'" (1 Sam. 8:7).

As a friend of the Bridegroom, John the Baptist also burned with the jealousy of the Lord. He had watched as the religious leaders of his day required the people to give their hearts to external rules and regulations. Religious rituals had replaced holy romance, and Israel had lost sight of the beauty of her Bridegroom. John's identification with the Lord's feelings for His people explains his zeal and why he was so emotional in his remarks toward the Pharisees and Sadducees (Matt. 3:7-8).

This emotional identification was also acted out very graphically in the life of the prophet Hosea. The Lord told Hosea to marry a girl name Gomer. Hosea loved Gomer, and for a time they were happy. They even had three children together. But one day Hosea discovered that Gomer had been unfaithful and had given herself to many lovers. Gomer eventually left Hosea, and the friend of God felt the sting of betrayal in a way he had never known before.

It was through his own pain that Hosea experienced God's grief over the betrayal of His unfaithful wife. Hosea began to comprehend God's undying love for Israel when the Lord told him, "Go, show your love to your wife again, though she is loved by another and is an adulteress. Love her as the Lord loves the Israelites, though they turn to other gods and love the sacred raisin cakes" (Hosea 3:1).

According to the Torah, Hosea could have had Gomer stoned. But the Lord instructed his friend to go get his wife and love her again. And if that wasn't hard enough, Hosea had to buy her back. But it would cost Hosea dearly. Apparently, Gomer had sunk to the lowest possible level. Since Hosea didn't have enough money, he had to pay for her with cash and barley (Hosea 3:2).

Hosea did bring Gomer back home from the slavery of sin into which she had fallen. He redeemed her, and their marriage vows were renewed. Hosea's pursuit of Gomer prophetically portrayed God's unfailing devotion to His wife. The Lord could not abandon Israel. In spite of her unfaithfulness, God would not forsake her.

God's word to Hosea had been, "Take Gomer back, regardless of the cost." The reason the Lord expected that of His friend was due to the fact that He planned to do just that with His wayward wife. He would pay the ultimate price to redeem her.

One of the most passionate passages in the entire Bible is found in Hosea 2:14-16. Speaking of His wife, the Lord said,

> Therefore I am now going to allure her; I will lead her into the desert and speak tenderly to her. There I will give her back her vineyards, and will make the Valley of Achor [trouble] a door of hope. There she will sing as in the

days of her youth, as in the day she came up out of Egypt. In that day ... you will call me "my husband"; you will no longer call me "my master" [my baal]" (emphasis added).

It's here that I believe the word *baal* has a double meaning. As Hosea 2:17 shows, the word can refer to the false gods of the surrounding nations. But there is another sense in which the word *baal* is used. Fifteen times in the Old Testament the word simply means "husband," but a husband in the sense of an owner or master. The baals were Israel's hard taskmasters, as well as her lovers. This is why the people gashed themselves to try to get benefits from the baals—just like the prophets of Baal did on Mount Carmel (1 Kings 18:28). When Israel chose a *baal* for her lover, she chose a cruel and merciless lord. Therefore, I believe the primary meaning of Hosea 2:16 is this: "Relate to Me as a loving Husband and not as a harsh master or owner."

I am convinced that Hosea 2:16 is a prophetic word for the church today. Because of the Lord's passionate love for His people, He is going to free us from the bondage of trying to serve Him out of cringing fear. He is going to reveal Himself as the beautiful Bridegroom and win our hearts with His love. He doesn't want us calling Him "master" out of the fear of punishment. He wants us to call Him "husband" out of holy passion.

CLOSING PRAYER

Father, in the Name of Jesus, my heart has been melted by the revelation of Your jealous love for me. Continue to renew my mind and free me from attempting to serve You out of fear. Give me the grace to live out of the reality of Your love for me. Amen.

Chapter Eight

PARADISE RESTORED

When the curtain went up on the first act of creation, God was in a flurry of breathtaking activity. He was about to "wow" the hearts of human beings with a world that was beautiful, fun, and full of adventure. If we stop for a moment and try to reflect on what may have taken place, we may be able to sense a measure of the Lord's happiness in all He was doing. The Bible tells us "the morning stars sang together and all the angels shouted for joy" (Job 38:7). We can only assume that they were taking their cue from the One who was celebrating all He had made.

The Lord created a man and a woman and set them in Paradise. He gave them a handmade wedding present (the world) and said to them, "Here, enjoy yourselves. It's all yours." He made them for intimacy with Himself in order for them to experience the undiluted pleasure of His love. And things could not have been better!

But shortly after the honeymoon was over, Adam and Eve ended up "sleeping with the enemy." As a result, God was *forced* to ask the first couple a very pointed question: "What is this you have done?" (Gen. 3:13). You can almost hear the pain of betrayal in the Lord's voice. The fall of Adam and Eve wasn't just a crime of passion; it was a betrayal of love. In love, God had created Adam and Eve, and they turned around and slapped Him in the face. They believed the serpent's lie, questioned God's goodness, and took matters into their own hands. And Paradise was lost.

Yet there was something about the heart of God that neither Satan nor the first couple could ever imagine. At the lowest point in the human experience, the Lord announced His intention to woo and win mankind back to Himself (Gen. 3:15). It was then that the story of God's pursuit of humanity began to unfold. But the devil still wanted center stage. He dreamed of being the main character in the storyline. Out of jealousy, it was his ultimate intention to ruin the eternal romance between God and man and turn the world upside down. Humanity grew worse and worse, even to the point that the Lord said of mankind, "I regret I ever made them."

But God didn't give up on His passionate pursuit of mankind. He started again with Noah, then Abraham, and eventually with Israel. He set out to capture the heart of a nation that one day would become the *womb* for Messiah. As the Grand Storyteller, the Lord wanted to introduce Israel to the eternal romance and the joy of what it would mean to know and love Him. This is why He used a very powerful *object lesson* to help her understand His heart and the way to Paradise restored.

THE TABERNACLE

God instructed Moses to build a tabernacle that was to be patterned after the tabernacle in heaven. Moses was told to place it in the midst of His people for all eyes to see (Exod. 25-27). The tabernacle was a portable tent that the Israelites could carry with them on their journey to the land of Canaan. It was used by the Jews as a place of worship during their early history.

In the Old Testament the tabernacle is frequently called "the tent of meeting" because it was constructed so the Lord could live with His chosen wife and teach her His ways. As the people contributed materials and labor, the tabernacle was completed according to God's specifications. The Lord blessed their work by covering the tent with a cloud of His presence and filling the sanctuary with His glory (Exod. 40:34).

THE CAMPSITE

The twelve tribes of Israel were told to camp around the tabernacle in specific locations that God had assigned to them (Num. 2-3). Each tribe was to fly its own flag (Num. 2:2). On the eastern side of the tabernacle was the tribe of Judah. The flag for this tribe depicted a lion of gold on a field of scarlet. On the western side of the tent was the tribe of Ephraim. Its flag pictured a black ox on a field of gold. Encamped on the south side of the tabernacle was the tribe of Reuben, whose flag depicted a man on a field of gold. Then on the north side was the tribe of Dan. Its flag pictured a golden eagle on a field of blue.

The symbols on each of these flags are mentioned again in Ezekiel 1:10 and Revelation 4:7. The lion represented a king who reigns supreme. The ox symbolized a lowly servant. The man represented the most superior earthly being. And the eagle symbolized the greatest heavenly being.

THE COURTYARD

The tabernacle was located inside an outer enclosure or courtyard (Exod. 27:9-18). The size of this courtyard was 150 feet long and 75 feet wide. Anyone could go inside the courtyard, but only the priests could enter the tabernacle

101

itself. There was one other restriction—the high priest was the only one who could enter the inner room called the Holy of Holies, and he could only do this one day a year.

THE COVERINGS

The tabernacle had two coverings (Exod. 26:14). The outer covering that was visible to everyone was made of badger skin. The color of the skin was a dull, unattractive gray. The other covering was directly underneath the badger skin and was not visible to the people outside the tent. It was made of ram's skin that had been dyed red. Remember, the ram was the substitutionary sacrifice for Isaac (Gen. 22:13). Furthermore, in the Bible the color red symbolizes the spilling of blood.

THE ENTRANCE GATE

There was only one way to get into the courtyard. It was through the *eastern* opening called "the gate." It is extremely important for us to be reminded that the first couple was removed from the Garden by way of the *east*. Furthermore, when anyone approached the gate, one had to have an acceptable sacrifice to get in.

THE BRAZEN ALTAR

When someone entered the courtyard, the first object confronting that person was the brazen (brass) altar. It was seven and a half feet square and four and a half feet high. The altar was the place where the people offered their sacrifices. The brass altar was also called the "Altar of Burnt Offering" (Exod. 30:28).

The Jewish people could not be pardoned from sin and blessed by the priest until they came to the altar with a sacrifice. In fact, the tabernacle and all its furnishings had to be sprinkled with blood. No one could approach the Lord except through the blood sacrifice that had been determined as acceptable.

When people brought their sacrifices to the altar, they were instructed to lay their hands on the heads of the animals and claim these deaths as sacrifices on their behalf. As the people killed the animals, a priest would take the blood that had been put in a basin and pour it out at the foot of the altar. The Jews were expected to approach God in faith, believing that their sins were symbolically being transferred to the animals. The slain animals became their personal sin substitutes. Even though the people realized that the blood of animals couldn't take away their sins, they believed the blood would cover their sins until God Himself would come and take them away.

THE BRAZEN LAVER

Another object that one would encounter upon entering the courtyard was the brazen laver. The laver was a wash basin about four or five feet high, filled with water. It was made of polished brass, the same metal which was used for making mirrors.

When Aaron and his sons were consecrated, or set apart as priests, they washed their entire bodies in the laver (Exod. 29:4; Lev. 8:6). This was a ceremonial cleansing. From then on, they only had to wash their hands and feet. The Lord required them to do this before they ministered at the altar or entered the tabernacle (Exod. 30:20). As the priests ministered before the Lord throughout the day, their hands and feet would get dirty, so they would come to the laver to wash. The laver would provide the water they needed for their cleansing.

103

THE HOLY PLACE

As one approached the entrance of the tabernacle, there was a linen veil of blue, purple, and scarlet. Once inside, one would see another veil that divided the tabernacle into two rooms—the Holy Place and the Holy of Holies. The outer room was called the Holy Place, and the inner room behind the veil was called the Holy of Holies. There were three pieces of furniture in the Holy Place—the golden lampstand, the table of shewbread, and the altar of incense.

THE GOLDEN LAMPSTAND

In the Holy Place, immediately to one's left, was the golden lampstand (Exod. 37:17-24). It weighed approximately 107 pounds and had seven branches. The lampstand was lit by oil. The middle branch was the central shaft that continually fed oil to the other six branches. These six branches, in turn, illuminated the taller, central shaft. The branches were trimmed every morning and evening to provide continuous light for the Holy Place. No natural light could get inside the tabernacle, so it was the light from the lampstand that enabled the priests to minister to the Lord.

THE TABLE OF SHEWBREAD

To one's right, directly across from the golden lampstand, was the table of shewbread (Exod. 37:10-16). This table was three feet long, one and a half feet wide, and two and a half feet high. Twelve loaves of bread (one loaf for each of the twelve tribes of Israel) were placed on the table in two stacks of six loaves. The loaves were then covered with frankincense. Every Sabbath the old loaves were removed and eaten by the priests, and the new loaves were placed on the table. On the table beside the loaves were trays and vessels of wine.

The table of shewbread, with the accompanying bread and wine, represented the covenant meal. When people entered into covenant with each other, they would share a memorial meal to complete the covenant union. The twelve loaves of bread and wine symbolized the entire nation of Israel in covenant relationship with God. When the priests ate the bread and poured out the wine on the Sabbath, they were actually representing the people before God. It was just as if the people were sharing in a covenant meal with the Lord. As the priests stood in the place of the people, they were also symbolically receiving the life of God into themselves.

THE ALTAR OF INCENSE

When the priests entered the Holy Place, the altar of incense was directly in front of them (Exod. 37:25-29). The altar was three feet high and one and a half feet square. Every morning and evening the priests would put burning coals on the altar. They would then sprinkle incense over the coals. When the incense touched the coals, it would fill the room with a fragrant white cloud of smoke. Once a year, on the Day of Atonement, the high priest would sprinkle blood from the sin offering on the horns of the altar, and then he would enter the Holy of Holies with incense billowing up in front of him.

THE HOLY OF HOLIES

The second veil separated the Holy Place from the Holy of Holies. This veil was so tightly woven that two pairs of oxen attached to each side of the veil and driven in opposite directions could not tear it apart. Behind this veil was a throne room in which God manifested His presence. Only the high priest could enter God's presence, and he could only do it on the Day of Atonement.

THE ARK OF THE COVENANT

The only piece of furniture in the Holy of Holies was the Ark of the Covenant. The Ark was a small chest made from acacia wood and was about forty-five inches long, twenty-seven inches wide, and twenty-seven inches high (Exod. 25:10-22). Poles were inserted into rings on the sides of the Ark so it could be carried by four men. The Ark of the Covenant was also known as the "Ark of the Lord" and the "Ark of the Testimony." The Ark was a symbol of the presence of God among His people.

The lid on the Ark, called the *mercy seat*, was made of gold. The mercy seat was the place where the high priest sprinkled blood once each year for the atonement of the sins of Israel (Lev. 16:15). Mounted on this lid were two winged creatures (cherubim), which faced each other with outstretched wings. In between the two cherubim and above the mercy seat was a blinding light. This light was called the *shekinah*, meaning the presence of God's glory.

Inside the Ark were the two stone tablets containing the Ten Commandments, Aaron's rod that budded with almonds, and a golden pot of manna. The two tablets of stone were also called the "Testimony" (Exod. 25:16). The stone tablets were given to Israel as a testimony of the Lord's character, His heart, and His ways. Aaron's rod that budded (symbolizing God's delegated authority) was placed in the Ark as a reminder of when the Lord's leadership through Aaron was rejected by some of His people (Num. 16; 17:1-10). And the golden pot of manna was a reminder of the supernatural provision of the Lord for His people in the desert (Ps. 78:23-24).

The Ark was carried ahead of the Israelites when they left Mount Sinai (Num. 10:33), when they crossed the Jordan River to enter Canaan (Josh. 4:9-11), and when they circled the walls of Jericho before that city fell (Josh. 6:1-20). The Ark of the Covenant was finally placed in Solomon's temple in Jerusalem (1 Kings 8:1-9), only to disappear after the destruction of Jerusalem by the Babylonians in 586 B.C.

The Ark served as a visible reminder of God's presence with the Jewish people. The mercy seat, covered with gold, symbolized God's throne and rule established on love and mercy.

THE TABERNACLE AS A PORTRAIT OF CHRIST

In its materials, colors, furniture, and arrangement, the tabernacle clearly depicted the person of Christ and the way of redemption. It represented in physical form the beauty and glory of God, as well as the ministry and sacrifice of Jesus on behalf of mankind.

THE CAMPSITE

The flags of the various tribes mentioned earlier in this chapter symbolized some of the unique characteristics of Jesus' life and calling as portrayed in the four Gospels. In Matthew, the Lord is depicted as the King of the Jews (the Lion from the tribe of Judah). In Mark, He is seen as the suffering Servant. In Luke, He is the Son of Man, the most superior earthly being. And in the Gospel of John, Jesus is revealed as the Son of God, the greatest heavenly being!

THE COVERINGS

In John 1:1 we read, "In the beginning was the Word, and the Word was with God, and the Word was God." Verse 14 tells us that "the Word became flesh and made his dwelling among us. We have seen his glory, the glory of the One and Only, who came from the Father, full of grace and truth."

Jesus is the *Word* that became flesh and dwelt among men (John 1:15; Rev. 19:13). The New Testament Greek word for *dwelt* means to "encamp, reside, indwell, or tabernacle." God *tabernacled* among men in the form of a man named Jesus Christ. In Him dwelt all the fullness of the Godhead bodily (Col. 1:19; 2:9). God's glory and beauty had resided in the Holy of Holies, in the earthly tabernacle made with men's hands. But the beauty and glory of God dwelt in Jesus, the *Tabernacle* made without hands.

The Apostle Paul wrote in 2 Corinthians 4:6 that the glory of God shines in the face of Christ. Paul even referred to Jesus as the "Lord of glory" (1 Cor. 2:8). But just as the badger skin veiled God's glory in the earthly tabernacle, the beauty of God was also veiled in Jesus. There was nothing outwardly attractive or appealing about the carpenter from Nazareth. He looked like any ordinary man. The casual observer would have never known that the Lord of glory was living among them.

Keep in mind, the ram's skin that had been dyed red was hidden underneath the badger skin in the tabernacle and was not visible to any outside observer. Similarly, the life of God flowed in Jesus' veins underneath His skin. His blood was to be spilled to take away the sin of the whole world (2 Cor. 5:19).

Through the New Covenant, Jesus would come to live in His people by His Spirit. He would no longer dwell in a tent in the desert or in some temple made by men's hands. His people would become the *tabernacle* or dwelling place of God.

THE ENTRANCE GATE

The gate into the tabernacle was on the eastern side. The tribe of Judah camped in front of the gate. Remember, Judah's flag was a lion of gold on a field of scarlet. Jesus' ancestry is from the tribe of Judah (Rev. 5:5). The color gold symbolized His deity. The field of scarlet represented the shedding of His blood for the sins of humanity. The tribe of Judah, its flag, and the eastern gate all pointed the Jewish people to Jesus, who said, "I am the way and the truth and the life. No one comes to the Father except through me" (John 14:6). Jesus is the way to Paradise restored.

THE BRAZEN ALTAR

The brazen altar represented the cross of Christ. As the blood was poured out at the base of the altar in the courtyard, the blood of Jesus was poured out at the foot of the cross. The cross was where the New Covenant was cut. The Lord gave Himself for mankind in self-sacrificial love.

Jesus, who knew no sin, became a sin offering so that men and women would become the righteousness of God through Him (2 Cor. 5:21). They would have the same relationship and standing with the Father that Jesus has. As a result, men and women would be able to enter into fellowship with the Godhead and have intimate communion with the Father, Son, and Holy Spirit.

While the blood of animals could only cover sin, the blood of Jesus took away sins, never to be remembered again. No more sacrifices are needed because the ultimate *sacrifice* has been made (Heb. 9-10). This is what Jesus meant when He cried from the cross, "It is finished" (John 19:30).

THE BRAZEN LAVER

Whereas the brazen altar symbolized the death of Christ, the brazen laver represented His life, which was consecrated for the work His Father sent Him to do. Jesus said, "For them I sanctify myself, that they too may be truly sanctified" (John 17:19).

Furthermore, the brazen laver represented the life of Christ coming into the hearts of men through the work of the Holy Spirit. Do you remember what Jesus said to Nicodemus? "I tell you the truth, no one can enter the kingdom of God unless he is born of water and the Spirit … You should not be surprised at my saying, 'You must be born again'" (John 3:5, 7).

THE HOLY PLACE

Christ was not only the fulfillment of the Old Testament sacrifices, but He was also the *way* to enter into the Holy Place. Jesus said in John 10:9, "I am the gate; whoever enters through me will be saved."

THE GOLDEN LAMPSTAND

Speaking of Jesus, John the Baptist said, "In him was life, and that life was the light of men" (John 1:4). In John 9:5

110

Jesus said of Himself, "While I am in the world, I am the light of the world." We also read in 1 John 1:5 that "God is light; in him there is no darkness at all."

As a man, Jesus was the *light* that would lead people into the passionate heart of God. He was the *revelation* of God's burning desire for human beings. He was the *perfect image* of the brilliance and beauty of God. He was also the One who would illumine the minds of men about the great lengths to which God would go to win their hearts so they could be in relationship with Him.

THE TABLE OF SHEWBREAD

The table of shewbread, which symbolized the covenant meal, pointed to the time when man would have communion with the Godhead through the body and blood of Jesus being broken and poured out in death. In John 6, Jesus said:

> I am the living bread that came down from heaven. If anyone eats of this bread, he will live forever. This bread is my flesh, which I will give for the life of the world ... I tell you the truth, unless you eat the flesh of the Son of Man and drink his blood, you have no life in you. Whoever eats my flesh and drinks my blood has eternal life, and I will raise him up at the last day (John 6:51, 53-54).

THE ALTAR OF INCENSE

In Scripture, incense is a symbol of prayer (Ps. 141:2; Rev. 5:8; 8:3-4). The altar of incense represented the high priestly prayers of Jesus on behalf of those the Father had given Him (John 17:9-10). The Lord was the only One truly worthy to petition the Father on man's behalf. As High Priest, He would one day present His own spotless blood before the mercy seat in heaven.

THE HOLY OF HOLIES

When Jesus was crucified, God the Father split the veil in the temple from top to bottom. The veil was no longer needed because the *perfect sacrifice* had been offered. The thick veil had prevented everyone but the high priest from coming into the Holy of Holies. But the self-sacrificial love of Christ displayed on the cross opened the way for man to experience God and to fellowship with Him. In John 4:19-24, Jesus taught that the day would come when His people wouldn't have to go to some temple in order to worship the Father. Instead, they would be able to worship God in their hearts and lives through the help of the Holy Spirit.

THE ARK OF THE COVENANT

After Jesus was crucified, His body was placed in a burial tomb. The disciples hid themselves because of their fear of the religious leaders. The following Sunday morning, Mary Magdalene and some other women went to the tomb to anoint the body of Jesus with fragrant spices. When they arrived at the burial site, they noticed that the stone that had been used to seal the tomb was rolled away. Assuming that Jesus' body had been stolen, Mary began to weep. But as she was crying, she discovered something truly amazing.

As Mary stooped to look into the tomb, she saw two angels, one sitting at the head and one at the foot where the body of Jesus had been lying (John 20:12). What she saw in that empty tomb beautifully resembled the mercy seat on the Ark of the Covenant. Remember, on the mercy seat were mounted two angels that faced each other with outstretched wings, and in between the angels was the light of God's glory.

As the fulfillment of all that was contained in the Ark of the Covenant, Jesus is the *living Word* written on the tablets of men's hearts (2 Cor. 3:3). He is the ultimate *representative* of the Father's authority, who was rejected by many of His own people (Matt. 28:18). And He is also the *manna* that came down from heaven to feed and nourish mankind (John 6:49-51).

THE TABERNACLE AS A PICTURE OF BRIDAL LOVE

The tabernacle was also a beautiful picture of bridal love and the intimate relationship that each of us can have with Jesus. When we are first *wooed* and *wowed* by the Spirit's invitation to be *wed* to Christ, we are actually being introduced to the way back to the Garden and Paradise restored. The Lord is the *gate* that enables us to enter into union with God and experience all He has provided for us.

As we enter into our covenant of marriage to Christ, we are brought face to face with the supreme sacrifice (brazen altar) given for us. The ultimate "bride price" was paid in order to *win* our hearts. Jesus gave His own life in self-sacrificial love so we could be one with Him and enjoy Him forever.

When we say "I do" to the Lord's proposal, we are then called upon to consecrate ourselves at the *brazen laver*. Immersion in water is meant to be an outward sign of being set apart for our Bridegroom (Mark 16:16). When we are baptized in water, we need to consider ourselves dead to

113

our former way of living. We have been redeemed through the finished work of Christ, and a new life is ours to share with Him.

As we gaze at the *light* of our Bridegroom (the golden lampstand), our hearts will be awakened more and more to His beauty. Meditating on the living *Word* (the eternal Logos) and all that He accomplished for us will create feelings in us that we never knew existed. As we continue to bathe our minds in the affirmations of His love for us revealed in the Scriptures, our hearts will be warmed by the revelation of His burning desire for us. The more time we give the Holy Spirit to change our way of thinking, the more we will mature in the love of our Bridegroom.

Just as married couples renew their wedding vows, each of us can renew our wedding vows with the Lord. This is best done by partaking of the *table of the Lord*—the communion of the bread and cup (1 Cor. 11:23-26). The more we remember His broken body and shed blood, the more we celebrate the marriage covenant we have entered into with Him. This is something we can choose to do as often as we like. The renewing of our vows with the Lord is something that moves His heart in the most profound way.

Intimacy in a relationship can never grow unless the two involved spend quality time with each other. In the same way, we can never grow in intimacy with our Bridegroom apart from spending quality time with Him. Just as lovers set dates and times so they can be together, we need to set aside time in order to experience the tangible love and affections of the One who can't get enough of us. The more we commune with the Lord in prayer before the *altar of incense* and allow Him to speak to us, the deeper our love will go.

However, prayer must never be viewed as a religious duty or obligation. It is not about discipline for discipline's sake. Neither is prayer about winning God's favor by telling Him what we think He wants to hear. Instead, we need to communicate with the Lord just as *lovers* share with each other. Prayer is about retreating to places of solitude and being transparent and vulnerable with Him. It's about being gut-level honest and passionate with Him when our pain and disillusionment seem to get the best of us. It's really just about being ourselves, knowing that His love covers us (Ps. 91:1). This is what shared love is meant to be.

Throughout the day, we need to let our minds drift back to thoughts about Him and His tender affections for us. This will enable us to keep the lines of communication open with Him. It is something we can do, regardless of where we find ourselves. Prayer is what helps us express our deepest feelings to the Lord. Prayer can be a tender word expressed in a quiet moment of reflection; it can also be a cry that comes from the depths of our hearts. However, when it comes to prayer, we have to move beyond duty and discipline. We have to pray from a place of intimacy and authority as the bride of the King.

For centuries, Jewish rabbis have believed that the Holy of Holies symbolized the *bridal chamber*, the place of intimacy. As we've already seen, when Jesus died and shed His blood, the veil that separated the Holy of Holies from the Holy Place was rent from top to bottom. Father God took the initiative in bridging the gap between broken men and Himself.

The Son of God left the *eternal place of intimacy* with His Father and the Holy Spirit and chose to lay down His life for His bride. As a faithful High Priest, he bore our names next to His heart as He entered the Most Holy Place of God's presence (Exod. 28:15, 17, 29-30; Heb. 2:17). He went back to His Father in order to prepare a *dwelling place* for us.

The *bridal chamber* has been opened to us. We can now experience a growing intimacy with Jesus that will sustain and strengthen us until we are with Him in the age to come. We can enjoy the passion of being loved by Him and the pleasure for which our hearts were made.

CLOSING PRAYER

Father, in the Name of Jesus, I want to thank You for the practical things You've done for me to illustrate Your passionate pursuit of me. I love being loved by You. I really can't get enough of You. Continue to lead me on the journey into Your heart. I want to live in the secret place of Your love. Amen.

Chapter Nine

A MARRIAGE MADE
IN HEAVEN

The Scriptures are a breathtaking record of the love relationship between God and human beings. While they chronicle the Lord's marriage to Israel, they also tell of a new marriage covenant for both Jews and non-Jews. The entire Bible is actually a marriage covenant, both Old and New. When the Scriptures are seen in this light, the need for understanding ancient Jewish marriage customs becomes even more essential.

The church has lost so much over the years by not realizing the significance of the ancient Jewish wedding. Jesus followed the steps of a Jewish bridegroom in taking a bride for Himself. Even though we have looked at some of the aspects of an ancient Jewish marriage ceremony, the more we learn about the wedding customs of Jesus' day, the more we will experience an added richness in our relationship with Him.

THE SELECTION OF THE BRIDE

In ancient Israel, brides were usually chosen by the father of the bridegroom. The father would, of course, act in his son's best interest. Quite possibly, if the son was old enough, he and his father would confer together in selecting a bride.

We, too, have been chosen to be part of the bride of Christ. In Ephesians 1:3-4, Paul writes: "Praise be to the God and Father of our Lord Jesus Christ, who has blessed us in the heavenly realms with every spiritual blessing in Christ. For he chose us in him before the creation of the world to be holy and blameless in his sight." The Father selected us for His Son. We didn't choose Him. As the Bridegroom, Jesus has always initiated love. The Bible tells us that "We love Him because He first loved us" (1 John 4:19, NKJV). He was pursuing us before we ever knew Him.

But why would the God of the universe choose us? He has chosen us because He loves us. And He loves us because He has chosen to. His selection of us is mysterious, but it's passionate and priceless!

THE BRIDE PRICE

In biblical times, brides were purchased. A bride price (*mohar*) was paid for a wife. The price was paid to the father of the bride, both to compensate him for the loss of a daughter and to show how much the bridegroom valued his bride. Sometimes the bride price did not include money or goods. In the case of Jacob and Rachel, the bride price was service to Rachel's father, Laban. "So Jacob served seven years to get Rachel, but they seemed like only a few days to him because of his love for her" (Gen. 29:20).

Although this may seem cruel and degrading in today's culture, it was actually a step above what was happening in the pagan world at that time. There was little or no value placed on women. If a man wanted a wife, he simply took her to his house, had sex with her, and she became his wife.

118

God introduced sanctity into the marriage relationship, and the bride price was part of raising a standard of righteousness. As a result, women were to be cherished and valued.

The idea of being purchased and belonging to someone has a powerful spiritual application. We, as the bride of Christ, have also been purchased. A very high *bride price* was paid for us—the blood of Jesus Himself. Our Bridegroom chose to pay the ultimate price because of the "joy set before Him" (Heb. 12:2)—the joy of seeing each of us redeemed as a spotless bride. We were the joy Jesus focused on both in the Garden of Gethsemane and on the cross.

The New Testament (which means New Covenant) mentions our bride price a number of times. For example, in 1 Peter 1:18-19 we read, "For you know that it was not with perishable things such as silver or gold that you were redeemed ... but with the precious blood of Christ, a lamb without blemish or defect." Our bride price is also mentioned in 1 Corinthians 6:19-20: "Do you not know that your body is a temple of the Holy Spirit, who is in you, whom you have received from God? You are not your own; you were *bought at a price*. Therefore honor God with your body" (italics added).

In Luke 22:19-20, the bride price is even mentioned by Jesus at His last Passover meal on earth. "And he took bread, gave thanks and broke it, and gave it to them, saying, 'This is my body given for you; do this in remembrance of me.' In the same way, after the supper he took the cup, saying, 'This cup is the new covenant in my blood, which is poured out for you.'"

When Jesus died on the cross, paying the bride price for His bride, He said: "It is finished" (John 19:30). The final

119

words that He spoke are taken from the Hebrew root *ka'lal*, which means "to complete" or "to finish." It is the same root of the word for bride—*kallah*. Could Jesus' last words on the cross have had bridal overtones? Was His bride His last thought as He paid the ultimate bride price for her? If we were on His heart, then why is it so hard to believe that we were also in His thoughts and on His lips?

THE BETROTHAL

As we've already seen in a previous chapter, the ancient Jewish marriage ceremony consisted of two main parts, beginning with the betrothal or engagement. The betrothal occurred up to twelve months prior to the actual wedding and involved a covenant commitment between the two parties. Once a couple entered into covenant with each other, they were considered legally wed except for the physical consummation of the marriage.

At the engagement ceremony, a marriage contract (*ketubah*) was presented to the father of the bride. This contract was actually a covenant that stipulated the bride price and other provisions the bridegroom was willing to make for his bride. Before the marriage contract was introduced into the culture, women had no rights, no security, and no guarantee of protection. The *ketubah* as a covenantal document elevated women to a new status in society. In the contract, the bridegroom promised to honor, support, and provide for his bride.

Just as the marriage contract contained certain promises for the Jewish bride, the New Testament (our *ketubah*) contains awesome promises for us from our Bridegroom. The New Covenant (New Testament) is a marriage contract

120

that shows us everything we've been given as part of the bride of Christ. All the promises have been given to us with a "yes" and have even been guaranteed by God's own "amen" (2 Cor. 1:20). This is why Jesus said, "And why do you worry about clothes? See how the lilies of the field grow. They do not labor or spin. Yet I tell you that not even Solomon in all his splendor was dressed like one of these. If that is how God clothes the grass of the field, which is here today and tomorrow is thrown into the fire, will he not much more clothe you, O you of little faith?"

The marriage contract was first promised to the house of Israel but was later offered to everyone. This meant that non-Jews who were once strangers to God's covenants and promises could fully partake of His love and blessings, including all the promises of the New (marriage) Covenant. Through this covenant, our Bridegroom promises to take God's Torah and place it in our hearts, not on tablets of stone, so that we might know Him intimately. Such intimacy is available to all who enter into covenant with Jesus and accept His *ketubah*.

THE BRIDE'S CONSENT

Although a wife was chosen for her future husband, the prospective bride had some say when it came time to respond to a proposed marriage contract. We see this vividly illustrated in the life of Rebekah that was explored in chapter two. Abraham's servant had met her at a well, and Rebekah had invited him back to her father's house to stay overnight. The servant discussed with Rebekah's father a proposed marriage between Abraham's son, Isaac, and Rebekah. The next morning, the servant wanted to leave with Rebekah and return to his master Abraham. But

121

Rebekah's brother and mother wanted her to stay with them a few more days. So Rebekah's family asked her, "'Will you go with this man?' 'I will go,' she said" (Gen. 24:58). Rebekah gave her consent—her "I do." To this day, Judaism teaches that marriage can only take place by mutual consent.

It is just as true in our spiritual betrothal to Jesus. The Lord never forces anyone to say, "I do." But He longs for us to return the love to Him that He so freely offers to us. The response He is looking for is mentioned in Romans 10:9-10: "If you confess with your mouth, 'Jesus is Lord,' and believe in your heart that God raised him from the dead, you will be saved. For it is with your heart that you believe and are justified, and it is with your mouth that you confess and are saved." This is the "I do" Jesus wants to hear from each of us. It's our confession of love and loyalty.

THE CUP OF THE COVENANT

When the terms of the marriage contract were accepted, a cup of wine was shared by the couple to seal the marriage covenant. The bride and groom shared the same cup, symbolizing the life they would share together. A second cup of wine would be shared months later.

In Judaism, wine has always symbolized joy. Marriage in Jewish thought is the greatest source of joy on earth. Wine also represented blood. The marriage covenant is a blood covenant in the eyes of God. If the bride is a virgin, when her hymen is broken the night of the wedding, there is a shedding of blood. Two lives become one in a lifetime commitment.

The cup that Jesus took at His last Passover meal on earth was the cup of the New (marriage) Covenant. Although the Lord was celebrating the anniversary of God's marriage to Israel with His disciples, He was also demonstrating that the New Covenant He was about to initiate would be sealed with His own blood. Jesus and His disciples drank from a common cup in an upper room in Jerusalem and became one as they drank the wine together.

But, remember, there were two cups of wine that were used as part of the ancient Jewish wedding. This may have been what Jesus was referring to when He said in Matthew 26:29: "I tell you, I will not drink of this fruit of the vine from now on until that day when I drink it anew with you in my Father's kingdom."

When we partake of the cup at Communion, we're to remember our Bridegroom, the bride price that He paid for us, and our marriage covenant with Him. We're to remind ourselves continually that His love is better than wine (Song of Sol. 1:4) and His affections for us are more precious than anything this world has to offer!"

GIFTS FOR THE BRIDE

The betrothal also included the giving of gifts by the bridegroom to his bride. Abraham's servant brought with him ten camels loaded with gifts when he was looking for a bride for his master's son (Gen. 24:53). When Rebekah volunteered to water the camels, she didn't have a clue that the camels and their precious cargo would soon be hers. Neither did she realize that one of the camels would actually carry her to her future bridegroom.

Many times a bridegroom would give an object of value to his betrothed bride to help her remember him while they were apart. Over time, the customary gift became a ring. The giving of the ring eventually became the main feature of the betrothal ceremony.

Today, a young man will usually give his fiancée a diamond engagement ring. When the young woman looks at the ring, she is reminded of the one who gave it to her. In much the same way, the Holy Spirit is our "divine ring" who continually helps us think about our Bridegroom. The Holy Spirit doesn't call attention to Himself, but rather to the One who purchased us. As the perfect bridal gift, He reminds us of our *Prince*.

The Holy Spirit is the greatest gift Jesus has given to His bride. 2 Corinthians 1:21-22 informs us that the Lord has placed His Spirit in our hearts as a deposit—a token of our bridal inheritance. Through Him, we are also given many other gifts as well (1 Cor. 12; Rom. 12). The gifts of the Spirit are really precious jewels that adorn the bride of Christ.

THE DEPARTURE OF THE BRIDEGROOM

Once the marriage contract was sealed, the bridegroom left his beloved to go to his father's house to prepare a wedding chamber for her. He would normally be gone for up to twelve months. During this time, his bride would prepare to leave her parents' home to live with her husband's family and become a part of their household.

When Jesus spoke to His disciples a few weeks before returning to His Father's house, He used an analogy with which all of them were familiar. We read about it in John 14: 2-3: "In my Father's house are many rooms; if it were not so, I would have told you. I am going there to prepare a place for you. And if I go and prepare a place for you, I will come back and take you to be with me that you also may be where I am."

Often, this statement by Jesus has been interpreted to mean that one day in eternity we're going to be given palatial mansions in which to live. However, these verses have nothing to do with luxurious homes in heaven. Through the finished work of Christ, a place has already been prepared for us. It's within the inner circle of the Godhead. It's a place of intimacy and fellowship that we can experience even now with the Father, Jesus, and the Holy Spirit.

While we are waiting for the day when we will see our Bridegroom face to face, we are not alone. His Spirit is in us, comforting and encouraging us. The following words of Jesus spoken just prior to His departure should really exhilarate us:

> It is for your good that I am going away. Unless I go away, the Counselor will not come to you; but if I go, I will send him to you ... When he, the Spirit of truth, comes, he will guide you into all truth. He will not speak on his own; he will speak only what he hears, and he will tell you what is yet to come. He will bring glory to me by taking from what is mine and making it known to you. (John 16:7, 13-14).

THE BRIDE'S CONSECRATION

The Jewish bride (*kallah*) was also consecrated or set apart for her bridegroom while he was away preparing her wedding chamber. The word *kallah* literally means "the secluded or enclosed one." This is beautifully depicted in Song of Solomon 4:12: "You are a garden locked up, my sister, my bride; you are a spring enclosed, a sealed fountain."

The bride belonged to her beloved, and she was to have eyes only for him. Her eyes were to be as dove's eyes (Song of Sol. 1:15). What do doves' eyes symbolize? They represent faithfulness, singleness of vision (doves have no peripheral vision), and loving commitment (doves mate for life).

It was probably easy for a bride to keep her bridegroom foremost in her heart and mind during the first few months after his departure. After all, she had the gifts he had given her to look at every day. But after some time, when the bridegroom's return was delayed, the bride might have been tempted to look at another man while she was at the marketplace. Would her bridegroom keep his promise and return for her? Why hadn't he come for her? Could he be trusted?

We, too, have been set apart for our Bridegroom. As we continually yield to the work of the Holy Spirit (the Dove), He will show us how to live lovingly committed to Christ. Because He is intimately involved in our preparation, our Bridegroom's reflection will be seen more and more in our eyes and in our lives.

We are the Lord's treasured possession. He delights in our being consecrated to Him. He wants us to have eyes

126

just for Him. Although He has not yet come back, we can be confident that we will see our Bridegroom one day.

THE MIKVAH

Brides in ancient Israel experienced a *mikvah* prior to their wedding. The word *mikvah* means a pool of living water used for ritual purification. To this day, Jewish brides engage in a ritual immersion in water as part of the physical and spiritual preparation for their wedding ceremony.

This ancient Jewish custom symbolized both a separation from one's old life as a single woman and the beginning of a new life as a married woman. It also symbolized a change in status and authority; a woman came out from under the authority of her father and came under the authority of her husband.

Immersion in the *mikvah* is a ceremony that has profound spiritual significance for us. Water baptism (immersion) is the New Covenant equivalent of the *mikvah*. When we are immersed in water, we are to consider ourselves dead to our former way of living. Upon coming out of the waters of baptism, we are to picture ourselves entering into a new life, lovingly submitted to our Husband—Jesus (Rom. 6:3-11).

THE RETURN OF THE BRIDEGROOM

A bride in ancient Israel had no idea when her bridegroom would return to take her to the wedding chamber. The groom didn't even know when he would go to claim his bride; only his father knew. The father was the one who determined when everything was complete and ready for the wedding.

Bridegrooms usually came for their brides late at night near the midnight hour. Shofars would pierce the silence of night. There would be shouts in the streets, and a torchlight procession would wind its way through the town to the home of the bride's family. This gave the bride a few extra minutes to make her final preparations. These details are reinforced for us in the parable of the ten virgins: "At midnight the cry rang out: 'Here's the bridegroom! Come out to meet him!'" (Matt. 25:6). The bride and her attendants would trim their lamps and prepare to meet the bridegroom.

After a bride heard that her bridegroom was coming, she prepared herself to be escorted on a bridal chair back to the home of her husband's father. This bridal chair is mentioned in Song of Solomon 3:9-10: "King Solomon made for himself the carriage [a portable chair]; he made it of wood from Lebanon. Its posts he made of silver, its base of gold. Its seat was upholstered with purple, its interior lovingly inlaid by the daughters of Jerusalem" (emphasis added).

A procession back to the home of the bridegroom began with the bride seated in the bridal chair accompanied by musicians, singers, dancers, family, friends, and bridal attendants carrying torches. The bride would be attired in her finest clothing and decked out with jewels.

Our Bridegroom has prepared a bridal chair for us. It has been built on His finished work of redemption. We are His bride, His queen! Even now, we are being escorted through the journey of our lives. The Holy Spirit is in us, providing all the protection necessary to bring us to our Bridegroom.

As the bride of Christ, we also have been clothed in His radiant righteousness. We have been decked out with all the jewels that His grace has lavished upon us. One day we are going to be presented to Him as a pure, spotless bride, blameless in His eyes (Eph. 5:25-27; Jude 1:24).

THE HUPPAH

The second half of the ancient Jewish wedding ceremony, the *huppah*, was also called the "hometaking." The *huppah* referred to both a part of the marriage ceremony and the actual room in which the bridal couple would consummate their marriage. The original meaning of *huppah* was "room" or "covering." The *huppah* of ancient times was a special room built in the home of the bridegroom's father. This is mentioned in Psalm 19:5 and Joel 2:16.

As mentioned earlier, the bride was lifted up in the bridal chair and carried to her waiting bridegroom. The groom always arrived at the *huppah* before his bride in order to welcome her to the place he had prepared for her. The bridegroom and bride would greet the guests gathered at the father's house and then be escorted to the bridal chamber where they would be alone for seven days. The marriage would be consummated, and the second part of the wedding ceremony would be complete.

The best man or friend of the bridegroom waited outside the wedding chamber to hear the voice of the bridegroom tell him that the marriage was consummated. This is what John was referring to when he said, "The bride belongs to the bridegroom. The friend who attends the bridegroom waits and listens for him, and is full of joy when he hears the bridegroom's voice. That joy is mine, and it is now complete" (John 3:29).

After the marriage was consummated, all the guests began a weeklong celebration. This seven-day period was also called the "week of the bride." This week is mentioned in Genesis 29:26-27 in the story of Jacob, Leah, and Rachel.

Over the centuries, the *huppah* was eventually replaced by a bridal canopy at wedding ceremonies. This canopy was usually a square cloth of silk or velvet supported by four poles and held up by four men. It symbolized the new home in which the bridegroom would live with his bride. The huppah was open on all four sides and symbolized the Jewish home filled with acts of love, including hospitality to strangers.

Today at Jewish weddings, seven blessings are chanted as the couple stands under the *huppah*. The end of the seven blessings traditionally marks the beginning of married life. The first of the seven blessings is the blessing over the second cup of wine that seals the marriage covenant. Although the blessing over the wine was the first one to be chanted under the huppah, the second cup is not taken until all the other blessings are chanted. Then the bridegroom and bride sip the wine, and the marriage covenant is sealed forever.

One day we will be taken to our eternal bridal chamber. We will see our Bridegroom in all His beauty, and we will experience the undiluted pleasure of being loved by Him.

THE MARRIAGE SUPPER

In ancient Israel, following the seven days in the *huppah* (bridal chamber), the bridegroom and bride joined their guests for a joyous marriage feast. The first meal that the bride and groom shared with their guests had real significance. The purpose of the festive meal was to instill joy in the hearts of the bridegroom and bride. The roots of this meal can be traced back to Jacob's father-in-law, Laban, who invited all the local people to a party after Jacob and Leah's wedding (Gen. 29:22).

The playing of music at the wedding feast was considered a duty. Flutes were traditionally played before the married couple, and dancing before the bride was a regular part of the celebration.

In the Book of Revelation, we are introduced to another wedding feast. It's referred to as the "wedding supper of the Lamb." It is depicted for us in Revelation 19:6-9:

> Then I heard what sounded like a great multitude, like the roar of rushing waters and like loud peals of thunder, shouting: "Hallelujah! For our Lord God Almighty reigns. Let us rejoice and be glad and give him glory! For the wedding of the Lamb has come, and his bride has made herself ready. Fine linen, bright and clean, was given her to wear." (Fine linen stands for the righteous acts of the saints.) Then the angel said to me, "Write: 'Blessed are those who are invited to the wedding supper of the Lamb!'" And he added, "These are the true words of God."

One day we will join the saints of all generations as we celebrate our marriage to Christ. He will escort us to the banqueting table, and His banner over us will be His love (Song of Sol. 2:4, NKJV). The music will be out-of-this-world. It will likely be one of the most powerful ways the Father expresses His joy over His Son having a bride that's suitable for Him. I can even imagine Jesus serenading us with love songs—songs that will awaken feelings in us that we haven't dreamed were possible to experience. Such pure passion and pleasure are beyond comprehension, but they will be ours to enjoy. And the celebrating will go on forever!

CLOSING PRAYER

Father, I want to thank You for opening my eyes to the beauty of the New Covenant. Jesus, I also want to thank You for the covenant promises You've given to me as Your bride. Help me to live life to the full—what Your death and resurrection enables me to do. Holy Spirit, I long to know and experience the comfort and security of my Bridegroom's love. Continue to melt my heart by the revelation of His beauty. In Jesus' Name. Amen.

Chapter Ten

THE BRAVEHEARTED BRIDEGROOM

I have to admit that my all-time favorite movie is *Braveheart*. I can't even tell you how many times I have watched it. I know this won't impress most of the women who read this book, but my life has been deeply impacted by this film. Although there are things about the movie that I could never endorse or recommend, there are several scenes that have left an indelible mark on my heart.

If you recall, William Wallace is the hero in the movie. Wallace was the warrior who liberated Scotland in the 1300s. When he arrived on the scene, the ruthless Edward the Longshanks was the king of England. Scotland had been under the tyranny of English monarchs for centuries, but Longshanks was the worst of them all.

Edward the Longshanks had issued a decree granting English nobles the right to invade Scottish weddings and to steal the brides away from their future husbands for the sole purpose of raping them. Longshanks had concluded that if he couldn't defeat the Scots on the battlefields, he would try to *breed* them out of existence.

William Wallace had fallen in love with a young Scottish maiden. Because he would not share his future wife with another, he stole her away in the dead of night and had a priest marry the two of them. As I've watched that scene over and over again, I've been reminded of another Bridegroom who refused to share the love of His life with another.

This is really the passion behind the *eternal romance*. Jesus arrived on the scene of human existence as a *baby*, but He grew up as a man who one day became the ultimate *Braveheart*. Although He has always been the *Lamb of God*, He has forever been a *Lion* at heart. To the Hebrew slaves in Egypt, it was the blood of a *sacrificial Lamb* that protected them. But to the Egyptians, it was the heart of a *Lion* that prevailed. As both a Lamb and a Lion, the Lord rescued His future wife from the "Edward the Longshanks" of the day.

JESUS—THE PASSOVER LAMB

Abraham's descendants had been living in the land of Goshen in northern Egypt for four hundred years (Gen. 15:13). When they first journeyed to Egypt, they were a family of seventy individuals, but they had grown to a nation of several million. Their numbers were as the stars of the sky and the sands on the seashore, just as the Lord had promised Abraham (Gen. 22:17).

In fact, there were so many Hebrews that Pharaoh, the king of Egypt, felt threatened by them. So he made slaves of them and forced them into cruel and inhumane labor, treating them more like animals than human beings. As time passed, the brutal taskmasters of Pharaoh's regime were more than the Hebrew people could bear. In their misery and despair, they cried out to God for deliverance. The Lord heard their pleas for help and remembered the covenant He had made with Abraham (Exod. 2:23-24). Because of the covenant promises, the Lord was more than willing to deliver Abraham's descendants from the bondage of Egypt and lead them into the land of Canaan (Gen. 13:15).

Although the Lord gave Pharaoh every possible chance to let the Hebrew slaves go, Pharaoh didn't yield. As a result, various plagues fell on the Egyptians as a consequence of their sins. The tenth and final plague was a scourge of death that killed the firstborn of every Egyptian family. The *destroyer* was allowed to pass through the land and strike the children. But the Lord gave His future wife specific instructions that would save her from the plague of death.

God chose Moses to be the human instrument who would lead the Hebrew people out of bondage. Prior to the plagues, Moses had been told that "This month is to be for you the first month, the first month of your year" (Exod. 12:2). The Lord was clearly implying that He was about to do something for the Hebrew people that would be like the first month of the rest of their lives. For them, life would never be the same; they were about to experience a new beginning under God's guidance and care.

This new life for the Hebrew people would start with the consumption of a lamb. The Lord further said to Moses, "Tell the whole community of Israel that on the tenth day of this month each man is to take a lamb for his family, one for each household" (Exod. 12:3). Every man was to choose a lamb without blemish for his household. He was to select it on the tenth day of the month, and then he was to observe the lamb until the fourteenth day to make sure there was nothing wrong with it.

On the fourteenth day of the month, every man was to bring the lamb to his doorstep and kill it. As he killed the

135

animal, he was told to catch the blood in a basin at the foot of the doorstep. Then he was to take a hyssop bush, dip it in the blood, and sprinkle the blood above and on both sides of the doorpost. There would be blood at the foot of the door, blood on both sides of the door, and blood at the top of the door. As a result, the entire entrance into the house would be covered with blood.

Since the Hebrew day began at six o'clock in the evening, the men had to kill the lambs around three o'clock in the afternoon of the fourteenth day in order to eat the meal by six o'clock. So when three o'clock arrived, knives flashed in the light of the brilliant Egyptian sun as the lambs were killed and the blood was spilled. Every family then entered their home through the bloodstained door. Safe inside, they roasted the lamb and ate it as they waited for the plague of death to move through the land of Egypt. Since the lamb had to be totally consumed, small families were asked to join with their neighbors so they could consume the entire lamb (Exod. 12:4).

Think of it! There were literally tens of thousands of men killing lambs, sprinkling blood on doorposts, and roasting the animals in fire all at the same time. The land of Goshen had to smell like one big lamb cookout! Imagine what it would be like today if all the residents in a city of 2 million people went into their backyards at the same time and grilled hamburgers. From miles away, people would be able to smell the aroma of the hamburgers and see the smoke from the grills.

This is exactly what was happening in the land of Egypt. As the scent of the smoke ascended into heaven, it reminded God of the covenant He had made with Abraham and the ram He had provided for His friend for a sacrifice.

The smell of the lambs being roasted in Goshen was further evidence to God that the blood of the covenant had been applied for Abraham's descendants.

Considering the Lord had also instructed His people to get ready for a journey, He said to them, "Do not leave any of it [the lamb] till morning; if some is left till morning, you must burn it. This is how you are to eat it: with your cloak tucked into your belt, your sandals on your feet and your staff in your hand. Eat it in haste; it is the Lord's Passover" (Exod. 12:10-11, emphasis added).

It's important for us to realize that the symbol for the nation of Egypt was a serpent. Throughout the Bible, the serpent represents Satan (Rev. 12:9). Just as God would use the blood of a lamb as the means for bringing the Hebrew people out of bondage to Egypt, through the Exodus God was also predicting that a day would come when He would use the blood of a *Lamb* to destroy Satan's power and set people free from sin and bondage to him.

As the Hebrew people walked out of Egypt, every individual had feasted on a lamb, and the lamb was in each of them. When they offered up the blood of the lamb to God, they believed they were symbolically offering their own lives to Him. They knew that the life of the lamb was in the blood (Lev. 17:11).

God established the Passover meal as an ordinance to be kept year after year, and from generation to generation. This would be an everlasting memorial to their deliverance from Egypt. It was to be the communion meal to remind God's people that they were in a covenant relationship with Him.

Now before the Passover celebration could begin, all the leaven had to be removed from the people's homes. The floors had to be swept, the corners cleaned, and the shelves examined. If the head of the home found any leaven, he would immediately remove it so his family would be ready for communion with God. "For seven days you are to eat bread made without yeast. On the first day remove the yeast from your houses, for whoever eats anything with yeast in it from the first day through the seventh must be cut off from Israel" (Exod. 12: 15).

The leaven represented the people's old life of bondage in Egypt. But throughout the Bible, leaven also symbolizes sin. When the head of a home would take a lit candle and diligently search every nook and cranny of the house looking for leaven, he was graphically demonstrating the importance of God's people forsaking their former life of sin and embracing their new life with Him.

When a family was ready to partake of the Passover meal, each member reclined at a table in a certain order around the head of the home. The head of the house was responsible for explaining the meaning of the Passover to the children. He would tell them, "It is the Passover sacrifice to the Lord, who passed over the houses of the Israelites in Egypt and spared our homes when he struck down the Egyptians" (Exod. 12:27).

God had made Abraham three promises when He entered into covenant with him. One of the promises was that Abraham would have so many descendants that their numbers would be as the stars of heaven and the sands of the seashore. God also promised Abraham that his descendants would possess the land He had given him. Furthermore, God promised Abraham that *One* would come through his lineage who would be a blessing to the whole world. The coming One would not only be a king, but He would be their God (Gen. 12:1-3; 13:15-16; 15:18; 17:1-8).

After the Israelites took possession of the land of Canaan and became a great nation, they began to anticipate the fulfillment of the third promise God had made their father Abraham. They began to look for the coming One. What better way could they look forward to His coming than by setting aside a place for Him at the Passover meal. They placed a cup at the end of the table; it was called the "cup of blessing" (1 Cor. 10:16, NKJV). No one could drink from the cup because it was reserved for the coming One. According to tradition, when He came, He would drink from the cup and cut a new covenant with His people.

Instead of putting the unleavened bread on a plate, the Jewish people started putting it in a small bag embroidered with gold thread. This bag had three compartments. Three pieces of bread, called *matza*, were placed in the bag, one piece for each separate compartment. During the Passover meal, the host would take out the middle piece of *matza*, break it, and pass it around the table. Each member of the family would then break off a piece and eat it.

The Israelites believed that these three pieces of bread represented their forefathers—Abraham, Isaac, and Jacob. The Jews would break the middle piece to symbolize Isaac being offered as a sacrifice. But they never fully understood the significance of this act because Isaac was not ultimately sacrificed.

When the Temple was eventually built, the people brought their lambs to Jerusalem to kill them instead of killing the animals at the doorsteps of their homes. The Passover was a time of great joy and celebration. As the

139

people sacrificed their lambs at the Temple, the priests would lead the people in singing the psalms of David. They specifically sang from Psalms 113-118. The singing was accompanied by trumpets, flutes, tambourines, cymbals, and other musical instruments. The sound crescendoed as the entire nation lifted their voices to the Lord and sang, "This is the day the Lord has made; let us rejoice and be glad in it" (Ps. 118:24).

As time passed, however, it became more difficult for the Jews living in the outlying areas to bring their sacrifices to Jerusalem. So the priests began raising lambs right in Jerusalem for the Passover sacrifice and selling them at the Temple. When a Jew came to Jerusalem to celebrate Passover, he could buy a lamb already set aside for sacrifice. It would be a lamb that had been closely inspected and found to be without any blemishes.

Picture yourself in this scene. You arrive at the outskirts of Jerusalem, the city of your God. You're extremely excited, anticipating the Passover celebration. The majesty of the Temple mesmerizes you. You find yourself moving with the masses of people as they make their way into the Temple area.

Somehow, in the midst of all the pushing and shoving, you're able to purchase a lamb for you and your family. You overhear someone say that there will be about 250,000 lambs slaughtered for the Passover celebration. (Josephus, a first-century Jewish historian, reported there were 256,500 lambs killed during one Passover.) A rather unusual feeling comes over you as you hear the sounds of hundreds of thousands of lambs waiting to be sacrificed.

There is a sense of anticipation in the air as the people await the festival of praise. There isn't much time left now until three o'clock when the lambs are to be slaughtered. So you move with the crowd as they head toward the altar at the Temple where the sacrifices will be made.

The priests are lined up in two long rows stretching from the altar all the way out to the people. Each priest has a basin in his hand to catch the blood of the sacrificed lambs. Finally the time everyone has been waiting for arrives. It is three o'clock. All you can see are the flashing of knives as the animals are slaughtered. As you cut the throat of your own lamb, its warm blood spills onto your fingers. Although it isn't your own pet lamb, somehow you still find yourself deeply moved by its death.

The priest standing before you catches the blood in a basin. He quickly passes the basin up the line to the priest nearest the altar. Very deliberately, the priest takes the basin and throws the blood against the altar. Then he passes the empty basin back down the line of priests in order for them to catch the blood of another lamb. It is then that you begin to rejoice and sing the great psalms of praise as you prepare for your Passover meal.

But can you imagine being caught up in the pomp and ceremony of the Passover period and never realizing that something of monumental proportions was taking place at the same time? Can you picture yourself missing out on the events that would be the very fulfillment of all that you had just celebrated?

Yet this is exactly what happened for many Jews during one such Passover period. It was the tenth day of the month of Passover, the exact same day the lambs had been set aside in Egypt. The true Lamb of God entered Jerusalem. Many people took palm branches and went out to meet Him. As Jesus drew near, they cried out, "Hosanna!

141

Blessed is he who comes in the name of the Lord! Blessed is the King of Israel!" (John 12:13).

Jesus, entering Jerusalem on a donkey, was fulfilling a four-hundred-year-old prophecy given by the prophet Zechariah. "Rejoice greatly, O Daughter of Zion! Shout, Daughter of Jerusalem! See, your king comes to you, righteous and having salvation, gentle and riding on a donkey, on a colt, the foal of a donkey" (Zech. 9:9).

But certain political and religious leaders sought to kill Him. For five days they observed and tested Him. Yet there was nothing wrong with Him; He was spotless and without blemish. These leaders could find no fault in Him because He was born to die as the Passover Lamb.

As Passover began on the evening of the fourteenth day of the month, Jesus was careful not to be seen around the Temple. He sent two of His disciples, Peter and John, into the city. They were to find a certain man who had purchased a lamb and prepared a room so Jesus could share the Passover meal with His disciples (Luke 22:1-13). But this meal was going to be different from any other. It would be the meal that ushered in the New Covenant.

The Passover meal always began with the head of the family taking a cup of wine and speaking a blessing of thanksgiving over it. Jesus also took a cup of wine, and after thanking the Father, He gave it to His disciples to share among themselves (Luke 22:17). But at the end of the meal, Jesus did something very unusual. He took some bread, broke it, and said, "This is my body given for you; do this in remembrance of me" (Luke 22:19). It suddenly became clear that the middle piece of *matza* bread that the Jews carried in their small, embroidered bag wasn't just representing Isaac and the substitute sacrifice. Instead, the broken *matza* bread pointed to Christ, the real Lamb of God, who was about to give Himself in death for the sin of the world.

Then Jesus took a second cup and said, "This cup is the new covenant in my blood, which is poured out for you" (Luke 22:20). He had shared one cup with His disciples at the beginning of the covenant meal, but He also shared the cup, "the cup of the coming one" (Messiah), at the conclusion of the supper. In doing so, the Lord was declaring Himself to be the fulfillment of all of God's covenants, including the Abrahamic Covenant.

Some time after the Passover meal, Jesus went to the Garden of Gethsemane to pray with His disciples. It was there that Judas betrayed the Lord and handed Him over to Roman soldiers who, in turn, took Him to the religious leaders. At the very time the Passover lambs were being examined for blemishes in Herod's courtyard by Levitical priests, the Lamb of God was being examined by the high priest and the court of the Sanhedrin (Mark 14: 53-65). The Lamb was later pronounced faultless and unblemished by Pilate (John 19:6), but because he feared the angry mob, he turned Jesus over to soldiers for slaughter (Matt. 27:23-24).

After the Passover lambs were found to be unblemished, they were prepared for slaughter at the third hour, or nine o'clock in the morning. At that very hour, Jesus, our Passover Lamb, was nailed to the cross (Mark 15:25). Then at the ninth hour, or three o'clock in the afternoon, as the people were singing praises to God, the lambs were slaughtered. It was at that exact time that Jesus died on the cross (Matt. 27:46, 50).

To perfectly fulfill the Older Covenant, not one bone of the Lamb of God was broken (Exod. 12:46; Ps. 34:20; John

19:36). And the Jews, not knowing they were further fulfilling prophecy, hurriedly took the body of Jesus down from the cross before six o'clock so there would be nothing left over for the next day (Exod. 12:10; John 19:31).

ENTERING INTO THE NEW COVENANT

When the Hebrew people began their new life with God, it started with the consumption of a lamb. However, it was just the beginning of a *journey* that was intended to lead them into all that God had promised them. Likewise, when we embrace the New Covenant established on the finished work of Christ, we also begin a journey. This *life* with God is meant to be enjoyed as we celebrate the *Lamb* inside of us and accept all that He has promised to us.

Salvation is so much more that a one-time experience; it's a *walk* that invites us to participate in the life of the Godhead. This is why we need to allow the Holy Spirit to renew our thinking about who we are in Christ and all that has been provided for us by the Father. The Holy Spirit has come to lead us into all *Truth*, and He desires to serve us by guiding us into our destiny.

God has given us all the resources needed to support and sustain us in this life, but we need to embrace the power of His Spirit as we desire to love and serve Him. We need to have our hearts awakened to the truth expressed by Paul in Romans 11:36: "For from him and through him and to him are all things." In other words, even our ability to love and serve God comes from Him. This reality is reinforced for us in Philippians 2:13: "For it is God who works in you to will and act according to his good pleasure." The grace of God teaches us that His

144

commitment to us is what enables us to be committed to Him!

JESUS—THE LIONHEARTED

In the story of *Braveheart*, William Wallace was the first Scot to defy the English oppressors. Edward the Longshanks, king of England, was outraged. He sent his armies to Sterling to crush the uprising. The Scottish highlanders had come in groups of hundreds and thousands to join in the fight against England. It was time for a showdown, but the Scottish nobles didn't want anything to do with it. Instead, they wanted a new treaty with Longshanks that would guarantee them more land and titles.

Without a real leader to follow, the Scottish people began to lose heart. One by one, they started to retreat. At that moment, Wallace rode in with his band of warriors, blue war paint on their faces, ready for battle. While the Scottish nobles were negotiating with the English captains to get another deal, Wallace ignored them and went straight for the hearts of the fearful Scots who had come to fight. "Sons of Scotland … you have come to fight as free men, and free men you are." He passionately reminded them that a life lived in fear is no life at all, and that every last one of them would die one day. "And dying in your beds, many years from now, would you be willing to trade all the days from this day to that to come back here and tell our enemies that they may take our lives, but they'll never take our freedom?"

At the end of Wallace's stirring speech, the men were cheering and ready to fight. Then one of his friends said to him, "Fine speech. Now what do we do?" Wallace replied, "Just be yourselves." His friend asked, "Where are you going?" At that point, Wallace responded with the famous words: "I'm going to pick a fight."

While the Scottish nobles were kissing up to the English tyrants, Wallace rode out and interrupted their little conference. He picked a fight with the English captains, and the battle of Sterling ensued—a battle that began the liberation of Scotland.

Like Wallace, the Son of God also picked a fight with His enemy. It began in the Garden of Eden when it was predicted that He would one day crush the serpent's head (Gen.3:14-15). Jesus had a battle to fight, and it was for the freedom of mankind.

The "religious spirit" has tried to remove the claws of the Lion of Judah and make Him out to be some nice, mild household pet for little old ladies. But that is not the Jesus of the Gospels. The *Lionhearted Lord* is the One who threw out all those who were buying and selling in the Temple and overturned the tables of the moneychangers (Matt. 21:12-13). His house had become a den of robbers, and in His righteous passion, He just couldn't stand it!

The *Bravehearted Bridegroom* is the One who, on more than one occasion, "picked a fight" with the Pharisees because they had placed heavy loads on the backs of His people but had not lifted a finger to help them. The religious leaders had undermined God's intentions for Israel so drastically that the nation had drifted away from her divine destiny.

In the Garden of Gethsemane, in the dead of night, a mob of men carrying torches and weapons came to take

Jesus away. They didn't even have the "guts" to take Him during the light of day. But as the *Lion* of Judah, He stood His ground. The sheer force of His presence knocked the whole group over (John 18:4-8).

When He made His way to Golgotha to be crucified between two thieves, he went as a *Lamb* to the slaughter. But He was a *Lion* when He conquered sin and death. As our *Braveheart*, He drew the enemy out and shamed him in front of everyone (Col. 2:15). And then with His last dying words, He cried "freedom," releasing mankind from the tyranny of sin and Satan, the original Longshanks. That one cry has echoed down through the centuries, liberating His bride from the pillage and plunder of her enemy!

While the Son of God will always be the *Lamb* who took away the sin of the world (John 1:29), He will forever be Jesus—the *Lionhearted* (Rev. 5:5). But to me, He will always be my *Bravehearted Bridegroom*—my passionate, conquering Hero!

CLOSING PRAYER

Father, in the Name of Jesus, I never want to be the same again. You've opened my eyes and awakened my heart to the beauty of who You are. Jesus, keep clawing Your way into my heart and ravishing me with Your love. Fascinate me with Your passion and conquer my affections. I want to be wholly Yours. You're my Lover and Lord. You're my beautiful *Braveheart*. You're my conquering *Hero*. Amen.

NOTES

CHAPTER TWO
PORTRAITS OF THE BRIDE AND GROOM

1. If you are interested in a complete study of the Song of Solomon, please visit S. J. Hill at www.sjhillonline.com.

CHAPTER THREE
THE FATHER OF THE BRIDE

1. Bob Phillips, *Covenant: It's Blessings, Its Curses* (World Challenge, Inc., 1986), 11.

2. John Eldredge, *Wild at Heart* (Thomas Nelson, Inc., 2001), 180.

CHAPTER FOUR
A SACRED MARRIAGE PROPOSAL

1. Marvin R. Wilson, *Our Father Abraham*, (Grand Rapids: William B. Eerdmans Publishing Company, 1989), 204-207.

CHAPTER FIVE
COMMANDMENTS OR A MARRIAGE CONTRACT

1. Marvin R. Wilson, *Our Father Abraham*, (Grand Rapids: William B. Eerdmans Publishing Company, 1989), 110-111, 166-184.

2. John Wesley, *The Works of John Wesley* (Grand Rapids: Zondervan Publishing House, 1958-59), 11:432.

3. John Shelby Spong, *This Hebrew Lord* (New York: Seabury Press, 1974), 31.

4. See Allen P. Ross, *Holiness to the Lord* (Grand Rapids: Baker Academic, 2006).

CHAPTER SIX
FOREVER FAITHFUL

1. If you would like to learn more about the subject of healing, you can order *God's Covenant of Healing* by S. J. Hill at www.sjhillonline.com.

CHAPTER SEVEN
GOD — THE PASSIONATE HUSBAND

1. Philip Yancey, *"What Surprised Jesus,"* Christianity Today, September 12, 1994, 88.

2. Darin Hufford, *The Misunderstood God* (Newbury Park, CA: Windblown Media, 2009), 53.

3. S. J. Hill, *Enjoying God* (Lake Mary, FL: Passio, 2012), 36-37.